THE POWER OF
YOU!

THE POWER OF
YOU!

How YOU Can Create
Happiness, Balance, and Wealth

Scott Martineau

WILEY

John Wiley & Sons, Inc.

Copyright © 2006 by Martineau & Associates, LLC. All rights reserved.

Published by John Wiley & Sons, Inc., Hoboken, New Jersey.
Published simultaneously in Canada.

No part of this publication may be reproduced, stored in a retrieval system, or transmitted in any form or by any means, electronic, mechanical, photocopying, recording, scanning, or otherwise, except as permitted under Section 107 or 108 of the 1976 United States Copyright Act, without either the prior written permission of the Publisher, or authorization through payment of the appropriate per-copy fee to the Copyright Clearance Center, Inc., 222 Rosewood Drive, Danvers, MA 01923, (978) 750-8400, fax (978) 646-8600, or on the web at www.copyright.com. Requests to the Publisher for permission should be addressed to the Permissions Department, John Wiley & Sons, Inc., 111 River Street, Hoboken, NJ 07030, (201) 748-6011, fax (201) 748-6008, or online at http://www.wiley.com/go/permissions.

Limit of Liability/Disclaimer of Warranty: While the publisher and author have used their best efforts in preparing this book, they make no representations or warranties with respect to the accuracy or completeness of the contents of this book and specifically disclaim any implied warranties of merchantability or fitness for a particular purpose. No warranty may be created or extended by sales representatives or written sales materials. The advice and strategies contained herein may not be suitable for your situation. The publisher is not engaged in rendering professional services, and you should consult with a professional where appropriate. Neither the publisher nor author shall be liable for any loss of profit or other commercial damages, including but not limited to special, incidental, consequential, or other damages.

For general information on our other products and services please contact our Customer Care Department within the United States at (800) 762-2974, outside the United States at (317) 572-3993 or fax (317) 572-4002.

Wiley also publishes its books in a variety of electronic formats. Some content that appears in print may not be available in electronic books.

Library of Congress Cataloging-in-Publication Data:

Martineau, Scott, 1961–
    The power of you! : how you can create happiness, balance, and wealth / Scott Martineau.
      p. cm.
    Includes index.
    ISBN-13: 978-0-471-79362-5 (cloth)
    ISBN-10: 0-471-79362-0 (cloth)
    1. Success. I. Title.
    BJ1611.2.M343 2006
    158.1–dc22

                                          2006005811

Printed in the United States of America.

10 9 8 7 6 5 4 3 2 1

Death leaves a heartache no one can heal,
love leaves a memory no one can steal.
                    —*From a headstone in Ireland*

This book is dedicated to the memory of Greg Walker, Timothy Ling, and Ted Korzenowski—great friends that left this earth far too early— and to all of those whose early passing, tragic or victorious, served to awaken and remind those left behind to live life to its fullest.

CONTENTS

Contents

ACKNOWLEDGMENTS

*F*irst, my deepest gratitude to all of the authors who honor the ConsciousOne web site with their presence. You have contributed so much to my life over the years. Thank you, Neale Donald Walsh, Sonia Choquette, Arthur Joseph, Ava Cadell, John Holland, Wayne Dyer, Sylvia Browne, Chris Howard, Marc Allen, Doreen Virtue, Gay and Katie Hendricks, James Ray, and the many others who will join us through the years.

Special thanks to Dr. Nathaniel Branden, whose work and mentorship have profoundly shaped the person I am today. I am conscious of his influence and contribution to my life on a daily basis.

Special thanks also to Morrie and Arleah Shechtman, whose guidance and friendship have formed the basis of my personal growth. I am equally indebted to their work and especially their books, *Fifth Wave Leadership* and *Love in the Present Tense*, the influence of which makes a significant contribution to this book. I have been so deeply inspired and infected by their work that I once jokingly told Arleah that I test positive for the "Shechtman virus"—a virus that keeps me strong, healthy, and growing.

My deep appreciation to the men and women of the Young Presidents Organization (YPO), especially the Santa Monica Bay and Bel Air Chapters, and the members of Forum 1—some of my greatest teachers and friends.

Acknowledgments

Thanks to Matt Holt, my editor, and his staff at John Wiley & Sons. I'm most grateful for this opportunity.

To everyone who has contributed to the success of ConsciousOne, especially our members, thank you; a special thanks to our staff, the best I have ever worked with, Paget LeBouef, Bob Crawford, Mike Shea—and to Robert, Tara, and Maddie, thanks for the fine start.

I would like to thank my family and deeply acknowledge the greatest teachers in my life, my parents, James L. Martineau and Mary Ann Martineau.

It would be impossible for me to express in this small space the depth of appreciation and gratitude I feel for my business partner and friend Steve Amos, the big brother I never had, the wise, old bull that put up with the young bull. ConsciousOne certainly would not exist if it were not for his vision, skill, and patience. Thank you, Steve.

To my daughters Paris and Melisse, who every day teach me the importance of being a father, thank you for allowing me to be your Dad.

Of most importance, I want to thank my wife Karen for choosing to continue to grow and remain my partner in life. The fun has just begun!

Finally, this book would not have been possible without the help of my good friend, Ridgely Goldsborough, who took my thoughts, ideas, passion, and enthusiasm and crafted it all into the words that grace these pages.

To all of you, and the many other mentors, coaches, and friends that have participated in my journey, I will be forever indebted.

Thank you.

Scott

FOREWORD

I must confess that when Scott told me he wanted to write a book, I felt a bit reticent. I remember the first book my wife, Terri Amos, wrote and the hours of angst, aggravation, the tedious editing, the lost sleep, and gray hair. "Not again," I thought to myself, but dissuading Scott is next to impossible.

I met Scott over 10 years ago when we were both CEOs of our own companies, waging the wars of commerce in America, rising to the top as we had been taught, measuring our successes and living the American Dream. But conversations over the meaning of it all revealed our triumphs and struggles, the underlying search for "what's next" and "what is the purpose of our lives." Together we began down a new path.

The wonderful thing about our business at ConsciousOne is that we are constantly exposed to new ways of looking at our lives. Many great speakers, teachers, and authors surround us. Each has his or her own approach and each resonates with people in different ways. Scott and I have learned that though the paths and approaches may differ, what matters is to just pick a path. Take the first step, and your journey will unfold.

One of the keys to this journey is finding your voice, offering a hand to those whose journey is just beginning. This book is Scott's voice. I'm proud that he took the risk. I believe his book will have a positive impact on many lives. I hope you embrace the lessons and enjoy the journey as much as I've enjoyed mine with Scott.

Steve Amos

THE POWER OF
YOU!

CHAPTER 1

The Demands of a New Age

Neither a wise man nor a brave man lies down on the tracks of history to wait for the train of the future to run over him.

—*Dwight D. Eisenhower*

*T*he pace of change has never been so dramatic or so fast. In the last 100 years—a mere blip on the human-existence radar screen—our tools and modes of transportation, our access to effective medicine and medical care, and our ability to communicate effectively over long distances has changed immeasurably. Our society has moved from horse and buggy to automobiles, from famine and plagues to abundance and longevity, from Morse code and the pony express to e-mail and instant messaging.

Imagine that you were born 100 years ago in the United States. Could you envision, let alone anticipate, the magnitude of change you would experience in your lifetime? Are you the type who would grasp the significance of the changes before you? Or, would you be among those who resist change—stuck on the horse and buggy as the "best invention of our time"?

There is a new technology changing everything right before our very eyes. Not everyone sees it—*just like the automobile.* Not everyone agrees as to its significance or sustainability—*just like the telephone and personal computer.* But no one can rationally deny its disruptive impact on society—it has caused seismic shifts in our lives whether we have been conscious of it or not. It has brought down governments, bankrupted companies, created trillions in wealth, freed millions, ended apartheid, and stopped genocide. This new technology relates to *information.*

Information once available only to the highly educated or the rich is now is at the fingertips of anyone who desires it. All information, every happening or event, discovery, or discussion, every bit of knowledge in recorded history and before is available for anyone who consciously wants it. This information is ubiquitous and easily accessible through your computer. The Internet has further quickened the already torrid pace of change in the last decade. The application of information as a disruptive technology, something so powerful that it literally renders its predecessors obsolete and alters the course of free enterprise, is only 10 years old—since the World Wide Web emerged in 1995.

If you have felt it difficult to keep up with world events, that's understandable. Even before 1995, the advent of 24-hour news channels, fax machines, and ease of travel brought information and understanding to more people than ever before. As information has become more usable over the last 10 to 20 years due to technological advances, the ripple effects for society related to the rate of change seem to grow exponentially.

Entire political systems have collapsed under this new weight of information. Governments unable to keep pace will continue to collapse. With more and more information available every day this pace will only quicken. We cannot cover our eyes or ears and ignore it. Our ability to exist, subsist, or flourish will improve or worsen in direct correlation to our perception and acceptance of this new reality.

Personally, I consider it exciting—the most interesting time to be alive—a time to create and manifest in many significant ways. I believe it gives more and more power to the individual — to each of us—to create exactly the kind of life we have always dreamed of. It removes the old barriers to entry to our own personal field of dreams.

The last 20 years have brought us a new era, aptly labeled the *technology age*. The inventions of the personal computer, printed circuit boards, microchips, cell phones, and so on, along with the Internet, all lend credence to the moniker.

I suggest that since 2001 we have moved into the *information age*, a direct descendant of the technology age. As with any offspring, the information age has distinct differences from its parent. Whereas the technology age made accessing information possible, the information age focuses on its applicability in ways that directly and significantly improve humankind.

Psychotherapist and philosopher Nathaniel Branden, Ph.D., considered by many as the modern-day father of the self-esteem movement, is a lecturer, practicing psychotherapist, and author of 20 books on the psychology of self-esteem, romantic love, and the life and thought of Objectivist philosopher Ayn Rand. He has sold over 4 million books in 18 different languages, and here is what he said to me in an interview:

> We've entered an information age economy, when wealth is no longer thought of in terms of land or capital or goods or factories. Rather it is measured in terms of knowledge, information and intellect. Nothing is more important than the appreciation of the mind in business, in industry, as the foundation of innovation, of discovering new, simpler or less expensive ways to accomplish goals. We live in a world where we need thinkers in large quantities, not just a few thinkers who give the orders and a lot of people who carry them out,

which was the pattern of command and control in decades and centuries past.

Today, if you don't understand that your chief capital asset is what you carry between your ears, you are in very big trouble.

I believe it is valuable to review how rapidly we have arrived at the information age. It is particularly important from a personal growth standpoint, if one is interested in personal growth, to acknowledge the past macroeconomic and societal eras and to understand how each era plays a role, consciously and unconsciously, in our everyday lives. A more informed understanding of the past gives us insight into what is to come and how to work with it rather than resist the inevitable.

Not too long ago, people lived in a primarily rural agrarian society. They cultivated the land and relied on large, extended families to work it. The family was the primary and sole labor force. With a high infant mortality rate, if one needed more help to till the field one usually sought to have more children. In large measure, survival depended on enough strong backs to till the earth, chop the wood, brave the elements, and make it from one year to the next. Not much thought was given to personal growth as hard physical labor held the key to survival for most.

The rural agrarian society gave way to the industrial era, characterized by a more urban environment with factories and metropolitan cities sprouting up to house the workers. Still, the ability to provide for a family was based on toil and strength, hours on the job, manning the assembly line and punching a clock. The primary mover of society continued to be physical labor.

With the advent and commercialization of the telephone we moved into the communications era, a time when human beings began to experience a new way of connecting, when information started to travel at a dramatically faster rate. Raw muscle played less of a role as the brain replaced the brawn, a transition that continued into the next age—the technology era.

Computers and microchips accelerated the move away from the high demand for physical strength. The ability to communicate with far-away lands made it possible to utilize the least expensive labor dollar possible. Work requiring high physical labor would be given to the country or company with the lowest price and best quality. No longer was physical labor a primary mover of developed societies.

In less than 50 years the primary method for gathering food, shelter, and clothing for self and family changed from an exchange of physical labor for wages to an exchange of service or information for money. Many discovered much power through their prowess of knowledge in programming, without any pull to work in construction or other manual employment. The mind's ability to reason became the ultimate commodity. The power of the individual's mental skill came to the forefront regardless of physical strength. The application of one's personal brainpower reached greater demand than in any previous era—with dramatic implications. For those able to make the transition, it gave rise to a time of tremendous personal and professional growth. For those less inclined, it caused great discomfort and difficulty. Either way, the inevitable and continuing change places great opportunity at the feet of anyone willing to embrace it.

To further demonstrate how the pace of change has continuously increased, consider the length of each era in the United States:

Rural agrarian age: 1700s–1849 = 150 years.
Industrial age: 1850–1940 = 90 years.

Communications age: 1941–1980 = 39 years.

Technology age: 1980–1995 = 15 years.

Information age: 2001–present = 5 years.

Morrie Shechtman, author of *Fifth Wave Leadership*, refers to the information age as the fifth wave of societal evolution. (His work in this area significantly influenced my interpretation of the subject and I am most grateful for his contribution to my understanding.) Reviewing the previous eras gives us insight into what to expect going forward with respect to the pace of change—what impact the computer and Internet will have on our lives.

It is further interesting to note what tools have been needed during each age. The automobile was invented at the end of the 1800s. The sputtering, fuming, cobbled-together pieces of metal on wheels that made up the earliest cars frightened many people and led these cars to be branded creations of the Devil. Those in the horse-and-buggy business scoffed at the invention and tried to have it banned because it scared their horses.

Think about all the ways the automobile has changed and impacted our lives in the last 100 years. Think of all the businesses that have been created—not just to manufacture parts for automobiles, but gas stations, road construction, maps, drive-in movie theaters, restaurants and diners, malls, hotels, motels, zoos, theme parks, garages, and so on. Imagine how different life would be if you had to walk or ride horses for transportation. Think of all the changes that have occurred as a result of this one technology and the speed at which they have occurred.

Consider another life-altering invention: the telephone. In my lifetime alone, we have evolved from party lines (where multiple homes shared a single telephone line and number) to nearly every adult in the developed world using a personal cell phone. Less than 100 years ago we still used the pony express, telegraphs, and Morse code. Today, I can call anyone in the world as I drive down a freeway at 75 miles per hour. The implications for your ability to create happiness, balance, and wealth in your own life are profound.

Perhaps more important than any of the above advancements are the commercialization of the personal computer and the Internet, for two main reasons:

1. You are alive right now and can take advantage of this era.
2. The opportunities are constrained only by your imagination.

Do you think that Henry Ford in introducing mass production of an affordable automobile knew he would be creating a need for takeout drive-in restaurants, 18-wheelers, interstates, and tollbooths? The invention of the car marked only the beginning—others besides Ford added their dreams. Consider all of the individuals who added to Henry Ford's dream, who used their own power to create products and services that contributed to the lives of many and led to happiness, balance, and wealth for themselves. Every one of them saw the opportunity and seized the day.

Much the same will happen with the advent of the computer and the Internet. The opportunities for you—for your happiness, balance, and wealth—sit waiting for you to take them. This is your chance to add your dream to the mix, in a world more connected than ever, a world where a programmer in India adds his code to a new software in Scandinavia that is evaluated and augmented by a young woman in Argentina and shared freely with all humanity—the case of Linux open code software, a global collaboration. The potential for self-expression and self-actualization is at an all-time high.

With great opportunity come equally great challenges. Nothing comes without a cost and one of the major obstacles that stands in our way is *scarcity mentality*. It's so important that I want to address it early on.

What is scarcity mentality? It is the mentality and mindset born of the Great Depression of the 1930s in the United States and the famines of the early 1940s and 1950s in other countries around the world. This mentality, this orientation toward life, creates a mindset of scarcity:

"There will never be enough."

"I will not get enough."

"I will be lucky if I get any at all."

"There is not enough to go around."

"Things never work out for me."

These typical mental statements for people of this generation became part of their imprinting that occurred during childhood. It is important to note that this mindset was required to survive mentally and physically at this time of famine and depression.

After the depression of the 1930s created a mentality of lack, the mental famine permeated the family dynamic on all levels and gave rise to an intimacy with scarcity rather than abundance, an orientation toward loss or fear instead of safety. This viewpoint was and is still deeply rooted in the minds of people of this era, understandably so since it was essential to their physical survival. Yet while they may have physically survived, the mental cost to their psyche, to self and family, has been remarkably high in most cases.

Since the imprint became so globally pervasive, it continues to be the mentality that many of us were raised with either consciously or unconsciously by our parents or grandparents. For example, the mindset of the parents and grandparents of the baby boomers to this day governs most men and women born between the period of 1946 and 1964.

Parents raised in famine or depression eras live imprinted with a mentality of scarcity that is passed on to their children whether they like it or not, whether they are conscious of it or not. This mentality challenged the traditional role of the father as a provider due to the uncertainty of where food and shelter would come from. It challenged the traditional role of the mother in creating a safe and secure home. Children worked as soon as physically capable, and taken out of school to address the prevailing scarcity.

Rationing and crushing economic circumstance served only to perpetuate the sense of inner starvation that has characterized a generation that to this day still wrestles with the notion of abundance, regardless of bank balance or net worth. Our parents strive to leave an inheritance while subsisting on white toast and chicken fryers. An unnecessary frugalness reflects self-denial and lack of deserving, a fear of "running out" as they did in the first half of the last century.

Fast forward to the baby boomers and post-boomers. In actuality, the last 40 years have been a period of tremendous abundance and plenty. In Maslow's hierarchy of needs, we have had our requirements of food, shelter, and clothing met for so long that they have ceased to be an issue. In just one generation we have begun to move from questions of "Will I feed my family?" to "What is my life's purpose?"; from "Will I ever find work?" to "What is my personal passion?"

The questions of this era and this generation are not the

same as those asked by our parents. Our parents and grandparents are woefully ill-prepared to answer these questions for themselves, much less for their children. How can a father who began work in a factory at age 12, 15, or 17 and worked there all his life answer a question from a son about how to find his true passion in life? How can a mother married at 19 to her first boyfriend out of high school give valuable advice to a daughter on how to choose a mate? This is the first generation where questions about the *quality* of one's life are paramount. Survival is no longer the issue.

Abundance mentality requires different models, different questions, and certainly different answers.

In the rural agrarian era, the soil ruled.

In the Industrial Revolution era, toil ruled.

In the communications era, those who could communicate faster ruled.

In the technology era, technology ruled.

In the information era, those with self-knowledge will rule.

Clearly, new models are required.

Because of the influence and imprint of our parents, however, many of us remain stuck in scarcity thinking or in some other equally restrictive pattern learned early on. This scarcity mentality allowed our parents or grandparents to survive an awful time in history. It was a model learned of the need to survive—when life itself was truly threatened. It is still part of the everyday mindset of our parents and therefore inescapably passed on to each of us. It is an old model that served its purpose a long time ago and now needs to be retired from active or unconscious service.

Unfortunately, without conscious effort the outer reality does little to alter the inner landscape. Without self-examination we quickly fall back into the scarcity mentality learned from our parents. We have to replace the old models of scarcity with new models—those that recognize the power and ability inherent in each of us.

Fast food, fast cars, and faster connections still leave us empty, without understanding, and trying to heal the wounds created by our adoption of our parents' mindsets regardless of the changes in the environment. We all fall victim to our childhood programming unless we consciously take on bigger issues, ask deeper questions, and probe within:

What is my life about?

Why am I here?

What do I want?

Where am I going?

What is my life's purpose?

What is my passion?

Automaton living went out with the demise of the industrial age. We don't line up outside the factory door, time chart in hand, in matching uniforms. The assembly lines have moved overseas and the historical kiss of death called individuality has taken center stage. We now have the freedom to express ourselves as we are—tattoos and body piercings, button-down shirts and bow ties, or shorts and flip-flops.

The computer makes it possible to work from home, to create virtual offices and flexible schedules. We used to sit in a cubicle or at our workstation and wish we were someone else and somewhere else. We have no need for that now. Our individualized brand has its own value that, if marketed properly, can help us write our own ticket.

The authoritarian, centralized command-and-control culture that drove agrarian and industrial society has broken down, never to return. It is up to each of us to do the inner work, to let go of old models and stigmas and replace them with new models and effective action to break the old bonds that hold us back.

In the age of information, self-information and self-knowledge become paramount. In fact, self-knowledge is the first step in manifesting *the Power of You!*

CHAPTER 2

New Consciousness
for a New Era

They must often change, who would be constant in happiness or wisdom.

—*Confucius*

Consciousness and Self-Awareness

*C*onsciousness, or the awareness of oneself, is a required skill to successfully navigate today's new world. With more and more information available and accessible to all of us, the need to bring consciousness into our daily lives becomes increasingly clear. With more consciousness we perceive more options, more opportunities, more paths to success, happiness, balance, and wealth. We also find more routes out of difficult circumstances. To perceive these new opportunities we need to live with more consciousness in our lives.

Creating a conscious life, one with true awareness of self, means pursuing an understanding of everything that contributes to our lives: our goals, desires, intentions, assumptions, and core values. It also means that we hold ourselves accountable for our behavior and actions related to those goals, desires, intentions, assumptions, and core values.

Most self-help books present a concept of consciousness with a California *woo-woo* or "feel-good" description. That is not what I am referring to. Consciousness is self-awareness, an understanding of self, not typically a subject addressed with much seriousness in self-help books. I want to draw this distinction right away as I am not talking about the consciousness of the world in general or society. Far too many books in the self-help arena attempt to address the concept of consciousness or self-awareness with soft and meaningless platitudes. I feel it is critical to bring up this distinction early in our discussion as it will play a particularly important role through the balance of this chapter and the rest of the book.

Creating Sustainable Change

In order for us to have the type of real result that most people desire when they seek to make an improvement or modification in their life, we must create sustainable change. Too often, self-help books foster an environment for short-term change but do not create an environment or an opportunity for sustainable change. Sustainable change, by definition, means one that lasts for a significant period of time and one that sticks—not the type of change that you practice for a few weeks, only to then fall back into old, less valuable patterns of behavior.

When I refer to creating sustainable change through *the Power of You!*, I am talking about providing tools that create sustainable change that sticks for the rest of your life. The first important component of creating it is to understand the difference between first-order change and second-order change. Let's look at a couple of examples.

First, let's consider the alcoholic who has finally decided to stop drinking. The alcoholic who uses sheer will power to stop from taking a drink is performing first-order change—

certainly commendable. Generally speaking, those changes that deserve to be commended and recognized are examples of first-order change.

Contrast that with the alcoholic who examines what payout she is getting from drinking. How does she actually benefit from drinking? Obviously, there must be a benefit that comes from drinking. Why else would anyone do it?

Second-order change comes when the alcoholic begins to ask, in addition to not drinking, what led her to becoming an alcoholic in the first place. She then begins to examine the underlying issues that caused her to drink.

The tough questions run something like this:

Why am I drinking?

What is the benefit to me drinking?

What feelings cause me to start drinking?

What is going on with me when I start to drink?

What patterns of behavior do I see?

What issues need to be dealt with?

Why am I hurting?

Why does this hurt so badly?

What do I need to do?

What issues need to be resolved?

By going through this exercise, generally with the help of someone who bears witness to the pain and suffering, the alcoholic can take on the challenge with new eyes. She can confront and resolve it once and for all, and create the type of change that resolves the underlying issues — not just the symptoms. This is second-order change.

Here's another example. Consider the person who suffers from obesity—more than merely being overweight—a person who feels the impact of obesity directly in his life. An obese person, much like the alcoholic, can decide through sheer will power to diet and lose 10 to 15 pounds. Again, while this is commendable as well as healthy, it still only represents first-order change.

Contrast that with the obese person who confronts the issue head on and uncovers how stress, food, emotions, love, and health play in his pattern of overeating. He then learns a new set of skills to cope with that stress and addresses the lack of self-esteem or self-worth directly. In that process, the person determines the value of leading a healthier lifestyle and stops overeating. This is second-order change.

Understanding the contrast between first- and second-order change when applied in one's life can give rise to fantastic opportunities. I am a big advocate for pursuing second-order change whenever possible.

Arleah Shechtman offers this point of view and example:

You need to get underneath the reasons that you drink or are overweight or whatever the issue is, and look at what purpose that serves or what decision you made early in life that you are still adhering to. I'm surprised at the number of people I know who call themselves alcoholics who started drinking at the age of 10 or 12. It's amazing, because they decided at that time that there was no other way to deal with that much pain. As a grown-up there are many other ways to deal with that much pain. That's second-order change.

I'm talking to a woman who made the decision at 10 years old to stand up for herself, and that's very unusual at that age. The cost to her was immense, because it's so out of the developmental sequence of life. The second order of change is looking at those decisions you made that served you well as a child but no longer serve you well as a grown-up, and learning or finding a way to make a new decision for yourself and to reincorporate that part of you we call the child.

There are, however, some aspects of second-order change that I want you to be aware of. As you go about creating sustainable change, you may find the change to be so dramatic that old relationships don't last. The reformed alcoholic seems like a different person to her friends and may have difficulty relating to people in the way she did while in an intoxicated state. The reformed overeater seems so chipper and bright that he seems like a different person.

We may find that we relate to people differently if we create second-order change for ourselves. Individuals who at one point in our lives were enabling us are no longer tolerated as friends. It is important to note that with second-order change certain relationships previously considered beneficial may become intolerable. Before we put the concept of creating sustainable change into action in our own lives, I would like to stress the importance of self-reflection and self-examination.

What Do You Want to Create?

It is paramount for each of us to figure out what we want our lives to be about, to consciously decide what our values, beliefs, actions, and efforts will be going forward. With that in mind, we need to lay the groundwork for discovering our own passions, interests, and values.

The process of self-examination involves asking profound

questions, probing questions that help us determine what truly matters most to us. Ask yourself:

What is my life's purpose?

What do I want to do with the rest of my life?

What do I want out of my adult relationships?

What kind of parent do I want to be?

Do I want to be happy?

What makes me happy?

What is important in my personal life?

What is important to me in my professional life?

What is important to me regarding my spirituality?

Only by taking the time and making the effort to consciously seek awareness of our true self can we begin to shift and evolve those areas that do not serve us. Only with awareness of these areas can we create sustainable change.

The great voice and life coach, Arthur Joseph, author of *Vocal Awareness*, when asked by me about each individual establishing their own unique persona, stated:

> We have an exercise in Vocal Awareness that asks us to choose our vocal and presentational persona. It becomes a template. We answer several questions. One, how do I believe I'm presently perceived, and two, how would I ideally like to be perceived? It raises an interesting notion that one actually has a choice.
>
> Part of the point is that we recognize an important metaphor, namely that every single thing in life revolves only around two things — to choose to do something, or to choose

not to do it. If how I believe I'm presently perceived differs from how I ideally would like to be perceived, then what does it take for me to embody the ideal persona, not in a presentational form, where I'm presenting me, seeking approval, etc., but in an embodied form simply consciously being the person that I say I want to be at a very core level.

As Arthur so aptly describes, each of us must choose to live consciously in order to become our truest self.

What Are Our "Familiars"?

To create sustainable change, certain definitions must be understood. The first one is that of the "familiar." For help with understanding our familiars, I am indebted to Morrie and Arleah Shechtman, authors of the book *Love in the Present Tense*, in which they define *familiar* as follows:

Feelings that have been with us since childhood, are our familiars. They are emotional patterns that we tend to fall into as adults, even though we are no longer living with the outward circumstances that first provoked them. Although we may have learned to behave differently as adults, we go on feeling the way we felt as children. When these feelings are triggered by something happening in the present, they seem perfectly natural to us. We have difficulty even imagining that there might be any other way to feel. Familiars— even when they are unpleasant—make us feel safe. We might not like what is happening, but at least we know what to expect.

In that same book, the authors use the following example to define a familiar.

When Greta performed poorly in a Child Beauty Pageant, her mother became cold and withdrawn in her disappointment. As adults, we may understand that another adult's disappointment is her own responsibility and that we are not to blame for it. Children do not understand this. Greta experienced her mother's coldness as abandonment and assumed, as children always assume, that it was her own fault. While preparing for pageants though, her mother lavished time and attention on her. Most of this attention took the form of fussing and nit picking. It was not exactly pleasant, but at least it was not abandonment. Although Greta cannot remember any incident from childhood that was particularly traumatic, what she remembers feeling on an everyday basis, was a kind of dull passivity as she submitted to the many demands of her perfectionist mother. That is her "familiar"—the feeling state that seems most characteristic of her simply because she felt that way so often.

When they first married, Greta congratulated herself on finding a partner who was the opposite of her mother. Where her mother used to turn frosty and distant when displeased, Dave got bombastic. He was loud but communicative. To Greta, this seemed like an improvement. His tantrums felt less like abandonment to her than her mother's withdrawal, yet she found herself still trying to appease her mother's cold sulks. She lapsed immediately into the feeling of morose passivity that was her "familiar."

The concept of familiars plays an important role in unleashing your own personal power. Feelings that have been with us since childhood are our familiars. In order to unleash *the Power of You!* and take advantage of this new era it is important that we examine, reveal, and understand this concept.

To create sustainable change we need to understand the feeling states that help us, and those that provide roadblocks or obstacles. Understanding what assumptions a child makes when growing up is important for us to grasp as these may form the basis of a familiar.

Let's return to Greta and her example in the Shechtman book.

It might not be immediately obvious that Dave, who has adopted the role of "Bully," has also found a partner who evokes his "familiar." His busy parents had overindulged his whims. When he threw tantrums, they found it expedient to give him whatever he asked for. They failed to offer what he did not know how to ask for, a sense of limits. For a child, it is frightening not to know where the limits are. Disliked by other children for his overbearing ways, Dave did not know how to behave differently. He concluded that he was just not a very nice person and resigned himself to the idea that he would always be rejected by others. While Greta grew up fearing that she would be abandoned by her mother if she did not win Beauty Pageants, Dave grew up feeling abandoned, period. Greta, in her reluctance to put her foot down when Dave bullies her, evokes in him the "familiar" childhood feeling of being out of control. When she sulks or cries and accuses him of being a tyrant, he feels like the person he always felt himself to be. He expects to be isolated and rejected and believes that it is his own fault. It is painful, yet irresistibly attractive in its very familiarity. Like most couples, Greta and Dave are attracted to the pain they feel when they are together. Why? Be-

cause it is predictable. If given a choice between unfamiliar pleasure and pain we have grown used to, most of us will choose the latter. The "familiar" gives us a sense of security. When you find someone who makes you feel lousy in exactly the same way you felt lousy as a child, you believe that you are made for each other.

Here is an example from my life of a personal familiar of mine: During the writing of this book, I experienced a number of interesting and unusual emotions. I discovered a familiar that left me almost paralyzed as I tried to express important points in the book. I felt unable to write, a little confused, as if I did not have the right to speak up and say what I wanted to say. I asked myself:

"What would my parents say as they read this book?"

"What if I revealed too much of myself?"

"Was I making sense?"

"Did this come across as a meaningful work?"

Very strong and profound feelings almost stopped me from working, and I understood that this was a familiar from my young childhood days. At four, five, and six, I was a tall, lanky kid with tons of energy, the eldest born to a young mother and a young father just starting out.

I was constantly asking questions, able to express myself clearly at a young age, and often, I was the person left responsible for the house when my dad was away on sales trips. I was supposed to be the man of the house, the one that took charge. I was supposed to be responsible for my younger sister and two younger brothers. I was not supposed to take the limelight. I was not supposed to grab the microphone or act out or express. I had to be there to help Mom. I remember that as the man of the house, I should be quiet and reserved. I almost felt invisible to my parents because I was never asked for my opinion or thoughts on things. I was just there to try and keep order. If I ever spoke up too much, I was not helping the family situation. I was told: "Be a good boy, be quiet, do the right things, do the things you are supposed to do and do not give Mom a hard time." I kept the house clean, so that when Dad came back, there was no trouble.

The act of writing became a challenge as I tried to express my own concepts and ideas, as I tried to speak out and claim myself. Even as I write these words, the feeling of needing to be quiet, to be seen and not heard, to not be challenging, and not be a truth teller, is my familiar. It was appropriate and allowed me to survive as a five-year-old, but does not serve me well as an adult.

Once the familiar was visible, I could shed some light on it, go back to my earliest memories, spend some time in that emotional state, and recognize that those circumstances no longer apply. This let me know that I do not want to be governed by those circumstances or that familiar any longer and that I do not want an obstacle to prevent me from sharing my truth. I knew that if I wanted to leave that old familiar behind, I had to grieve the loss of the child-like fun or the truth teller that I was back then—the one that was not honored or appreciated by my parents.

I had to mourn that loss and understand that I experienced a form of abandonment—that my parents were not there for me in a way that I needed them to be. I had to recognize that I made some decisions based on that abandonment and believed that I was alone.

I thought that I could not trust other people or that people did not want to hear the truth. Because of my family situations, because of my family circumstances, I did not have the experience of someone saying "yes, please speak the truth, please tell the truth."

Few people do. Most children experience times when their needs are left unmet—especially in the transitional and separation phases—when children begin to understand that they are not their parents. Though most of us intellectually know this as adults, as a child, the abandonment is experienced as a form of death. A three- or four-year-old barely comprehends the notion that he or she is separate from his or her parents. The familiar is that the parents are the child's whole life. Naturally, a form of abandonment is experienced and becomes part of the eventual maturation process required for survival in this world.

The conclusions we draw as a result of unmet needs in childhood form the basis of a major issue for most of us as adults. While valid as a baby, these same conclusions may not be as productive for your life as an adult. It is not about blaming your parents but rather about understanding that needs were not met, recalling the conclusions made at that time, and recognizing whether those conclusions help or hurt in your present life situation.

As I started to write this book, these old familiars came up. I understand what purpose they served in the past and how they no longer serve today. I have processed my own grief, mourned the loss of not being heard, and felt the uncomfortable feeling that goes along with lifting such a heavy burden.

There are still times when I feel like a tall poppy that is going to be cut down because I have stuck my head up too high or spoken out too much. Now, because of my understanding of that familiar, I am able to check in with myself and decide, does this notion serve me today? Is this a present reality or is this something that I understood as a child that no longer helps me? Understanding that familiar has unleashed my power, unleashed my ability to be more of the person that I need to be.

In this new era, we all need a new level of consciousness— an awareness of our past, an understanding of the present, and a clear vision for our future.

CHAPTER 3

Choosing Your Core Values

Happiness is that state of consciousness which proceeds from the achievement of one's values.

—*Ayn Rand*

*I*n order to actualize our lives and find happiness, balance, and wealth, we have to first identify who we are and what we stand for. We need to clarify and declare our core values.

Many people define core values in different ways. For the purposes of this book, we will use the following definitions:

- *Core values are key, basic, or central values that integrate a person.* Core values are defined as the essential, enduring tests of a person's belief system. This small set of principles has a profound influence on how a person thinks and acts. When following these core values, actions require no external justification. These principles have intrinsic value and are of significant importance—a few powerful guidelines that define the person, who they are and what they

---

Once again, I'm indebted to Morrie and Arleah Shechtman and their book, *Love in the Present Tense*, which provides the basis for my understanding of core values.

do. These values give the person a lasting identity, and provide the glue that holds a person together.

- *Core values are constant.* Core values change very slowly if at all. Consequently, it is critical to begin with the right ones.

- *Core values are passionate. Vision* is a seeing word, *passion* is a feeling word. Core values touch the heart and elicit strong emotions. They stir feelings that move people to action.

- *Core values are core beliefs.* People often use various synonyms for values: *precepts, principles, tenets, standards,* or *assumptions,* some of which may not accurately equate. Values are primary or core beliefs. A belief is a conviction or opinion you hold true based on evidence or proof.

Arleah Shechtman states the following:

Whatever else is true in life, most of our decisions and paths basically come from our core values. Many things happen as we're growing up, a lot of compromises and twisting of our core values. Our task as adults is to sort that all out. For example, if you have a core value of personal responsibility, then that makes decisions much easier than if you're not clear about that value. If sometimes you're responsible and sometimes you are not, that makes life confusing and difficult. The importance of articulating our core values is not only so that we can lead a coherent life, but also to enable us to move through all the information that we're bombarded with. Sometimes in our families there is a clash of core values, and that clash is the root of most of our emotional pain and struggle.

There are many core values and only you can define your own. Because this process is so critical to actualizing *the Power of You!,* I am including a number of possibilities for you to consider. You will notice that many core values contain elements of other core values within them. Most core values make sense and you will likely agree that they are excellent principles to live by.

However, the only way that you should consider any of them a true core value is if they influence your daily activities in a meaningful way. In other words, you base your decisions on those values, even when you have to make an unwanted sacrifice. You choose a value, declare it to be your own, and pay the necessary price to live by it.

Let's examine 16 common core values. Below each definition, I have included a series of questions to help you identify your core values.

1. *Honesty.* Honesty means to consistently seek and speak the truth. It involves living a lifestyle without lying, cheating, stealing, or other forms of deception, consciously or unconsciously. Honesty demands a proactive approach to develop the muscle that naturally lives in truth, without effort or strain.

   Consider these questions:

   - Does your daily life consist of authentic statements regarding who you are and what you are trying to do?
   - Is what you say and do in alignment with who you say you are?
   - How do you feel about "little white lies"?

2. *Respect.* Respect means to value self, others, and property, both real and personal. It includes the ability to un-

derstand where your rights end and someone else's be-gin. Respect shows appreciation for sacrifices that have been made for your benefit.

Consider these questions:

- Do you treat your own feelings with respect?

- Do you honor your feelings, thoughts, and desires by acting on them each day?

- Do you keep your commitments to yourself and others?

3. *Reason or rationality.* Reason and rationality means to demonstrate a capacity for understanding and a bias toward logical, rational, and analytical thought. It in-volves the active use of our intelligence. It includes a proclivity for consistent good judgment and sound, common sense.

Consider these questions:

- In the last year, have you avoided poor outcomes be-cause something you were presented with simply didn't make sense?

- Have you pursued a path or goal based on sound logi-cal thinking?

- Do you surround yourself with people who often don't make sense or gravitate toward those who challenge you with a strong intellect?

4. *Compassion.* Compassion means to show care and kind-ness for others. It includes the courage to confront oth-ers and speak the truth, to say what needs to be said. A compassionate person helps others in need, often with-out visible or tangible reward.

Consider these questions:

- Are you kind to yourself and others?

- Are your "self-talk" and your interactions with others positive and affirming?

- Do you provide feedback that is helpful or just what the person wants to hear?

5. *Courage.* Courage means to face difficult situations with confidence and determination. A courageous person stands up for her convictions when conscience demands. A courageous person does not shy away from difficulties but rather consciously chooses to confront issues despite whatever challenges may exist.

Consider these questions:

- Do you persevere when change is required?

- Do you make the tough calls when it comes to your personal life?

- In what ways have you stood up for yourself or others, when it was required of you?

6. *Self-Disclosure.* Self-disclosure means to continuously and consistently reveal and uncover who you are to yourself and others. Self-disclosure is both the conscious and unconscious act of revealing more about yourself to others. This may include, but is not limited to, thoughts, feelings, aspirations, goals, failures, successes, fears, and dreams, as well as likes and dislikes. Many people attempt to avoid self-disclosing too much to co-workers, or when dating, for fear of being judged negatively.

Consider these questions:

- Do you risk self-disclosure with people in your daily life?
- Are you continuously revealing who you truly are with others, or do you hide when presented with an opportunity to do so?
- Do you let people know how you feel, share your excitement, happiness, sadness, or anger, or do you keep those feelings to yourself?

7. *Good citizenship.* A good citizen is a productive and contributing member of society. A good citizen is not a taker or freeloader. A good citizen understands the importance of abiding by the law and the rules of order commonly understood by the community. A good citizen does not hesitate to help a neighbor and participate in civic activities.

    Consider these questions:

- In what ways over the last year have you contributed to your community?
- How has the community benefited from your involvement?
- Is there something more your community needs from you and/or something you can't wait to do for your community?

8. *Industriousness.* The industrious person realizes the intrinsic and extrinsic rewards of putting forth efforts to achieve goals. In addition to understanding the rewards, the industrious person takes the action necessary to go after them. He takes responsibility for results and shows a determination to find a way to make results happen.

Consider these questions:

- Is your work fun?

- Does your mind sometimes race with ideas for your work, where you literally get lost in it and lose track of time?

- What is the work you do all about and why do you do it—is it financially rewarding, personally rewarding, or both?

9. *Personal health.* Healthy people pay attention to what they put into their body. They take care of their weight, pay attention to cholesterol and blood pressure, understand the need for routine checkups and do them. They take responsibility for governing themselves when it comes to temperance in diet, getting a proper amount of sleep, maintaining an exercise regime, and so on. Healthy people do not make excuses for why they can't find time to take care of themselves nor do they blame anyone else for how they feel.

Consider these questions:

- How well do you eat and do you even know what that means?

- Do you exercise regularly?

- Would you rather spend time outside in recreational activities or watch television to relax?

10. *Personal growth.* Personal growth means the continual process of learning about yourself, expanding your point of view, and extending yourself into the world. People committed to personal growth constantly ask themselves why they do what they do and feel what they feel. When

confronted with setbacks, they are eager to explore what has gone wrong and how to do better next time. When they find themselves in conflict with others, they are interested in learning what the conflict has to teach them about themselves. They take risks and try out new behaviors. They don't consider themselves a finished product. They expect to keep changing right up to the moment they breathe their last breath.

Consider these questions:

- Over the past year, what have you worked hardest to change or develop in yourself?

- Of what recent personal growth achievement are you most proud?

- What do you regularly do to continue your own personal growth?

11. *Willingness to challenge another.* You care most for others when you demand that they become the best they can be. In relationships where mutual challenge is a value, it is not acceptable for either person to fall into a protracted slump. Each party holds the other accountable for living up to his best vision of himself and for continuing to grow. Challenge is a vote of confidence, a sign of respect.

In an interview, Dr. Nathaniel Branden expressed this point as follows:

> *You might also include the desirability of trying to talk always to a person's best self, to address the most balanced, the most rational, the most compassionate, the most civilized, the best within the person, from which the person him- or herself sometimes can get*

alienated. We need to retain our vision that that exists in the person and speak to it.

You hold a high expectation of people succeeding and overcoming and don't shy away from sharing that even though the road is bumpy, you will persevere, that you will overcome.

Conversely, accepting people exactly as they are is a form of abandonment. When you don't challenge another person, then you are essentially giving up on them.

Consider these questions:

- Your significant other, who used to be very outgoing and active, has lately turned into a couch potato and has begun to put on a lot of weight. What do you do?

- When faced with a challenging issue that needs addressing, do you confront it or avoid it?

- When someone points out something about your actions or behavior, do you listen or do you immediately go on the defensive?

In an interview, Arthur Joseph highlighted the benefit of challenging another through his description of his own work:

I teach complete surrender—though not to me. I want no dominion over a client or a student. The surrender is to the work, the capital "W" work and at a deeper level to source, however we identify that to be. The root of the word surrender means to yield or to give back. We're in service to our mission, to our persona, to our goals, to that which we say we want to do and be in the world.

Toward that end, I am the sand in the oyster shell. I challenge you to be the best of yourself possible, not to be perfect, but to be excellent. Perfect doesn't let us mess up. Excellence allows us to make mistakes, fall, pick ourselves up, and still strive to serve that greater good, that greater sense of self.

12. *Preeminence of the adult relationship.* This is a particularly critical core value for married couples with children. Marriage works best when it is given a higher priority than any other relationship in either partner's life. All other relationships — including those with friends, family of origin, and children should come second. Relationships with children are necessarily lacking in reciprocity. The adult gives more than the child can reasonably be expected to return. No child is capable of meeting an adult's needs for intimacy. The unmet needs of adults who neglect their marriages in an excessive focus on parenting become a terrible burden on their children. The children feel responsible for making their parents happy and end up blaming themselves for the deterioration of the adult relationship.

    Consider these questions:

    - Do you feel like the most important person in your significant other's life?
    - If not, who do you believe comes before you?
    - Is your significant other the most important person in your life?
    - If not, who comes before them?

13. *Dedication to life's purpose.* Most of us are deeply committed to and actively involved in some endeavor or another. Most often this is a person's career, but what you are dedicated to matters less than being dedicated to

something that gives your life meaning and purpose, something that demands all-out effort and the fullest expression of your talents and values. No matter how fat the paycheck, you are not a full person if your paycheck is all that you have to show at the end of the day. It is important to devote our lives to something that we truly care about.

Consider these questions:

• Would you give up your safe position to go after the dream job with a new company even if it means a temporary pay cut and a risk that the enterprise won't make it?

• What's more important to you, personal fulfillment or comfort?

• How far will you go to live your passion, to reject any endeavor that does not align with your life's purpose, even if that act causes conflict with your closest relationships?

Dr. Branden offers the following regarding this core value, from the perspective of his own work:

> *The need, the desirability of having something central to your life, for which you are fully accountable, and you are willing and able to stay focused on and deal with purposefully is absolute. It's not enough to have glorious goals or great aspirations. If we don't also have the ability to focus, the discipline to stay on purpose with regard to the achievement of those goals or dreams, they aren't really goals, they're just daydreams.*
>
> *One of the most important tasks in the work that I do, either in psychotherapy or in life coaching, is to*

help people become aware of and articulate the goals and dreams which may be completely submerged, and therefore never get handled or acted on appropriately. Even ahead of knowing what to do, is the need to know what the target is, what the mission is, what the goal is, what the dream is, what the aspiration is.

14. *Inner renewal.* Inner renewal might also be called "spirituality." This involves a consistent tapping into some source of inner renewal. For some people this is accomplished through religious services or practices like meditation, but it can also come from the enjoyment of nature or art, exercise or hobbies, journaling, or spending quiet time alone with oneself. When you care for yourself in this way, you stay in touch with your own inner life, replenish your energy, put everyday hassles into perspective, and gain the strength to pull through crises.
    Consider these questions:

    • What practices or activities give you a sense of inner renewal?

    • Of these activities, which is the most important to you and when was the last time that you did the activity that you selected as most important?

    • When you're feeling completely drained, what do you do to recharge your batteries?

15. *Accountability.* All of us are accountable for our actions and the impact of those actions. Accountability means keeping one's word, following through on commitments, telling the truth, and accepting the full consequences of what we do and neglect to do. Accountability involves your ability to account for yourself, to measure

what you do and understand that only results, not good intentions, make a difference.

Consider these questions:

- You call in sick from work and go fishing. When asked at work the next day where you were, what do you say?

- Your team is responsible for bringing in a project on time. You do your part but others don't. Whom do you blame?

- If you have a target, do you go the extra mile to hit it—seldom, sometimes, always?

Dr. Branden made this statement about accountability:

> *We are the author of our choices and actions. We are responsible for our life and wellbeing. We are accountable for our promises, our commitments, and without that, you can't have a successful life. You can't experience self-respect. You can't inspire the respect of others. And you won't reach for the realization of your dreams.*

16. *Quality communication.* Quality communication is a value that flows both ways. It includes both a commitment to sharing one's own life with others as well as a commitment to listening with full attention to others. It means opening up and creating intimacy in communication, revealing oneself with courage. It also means staying open to the communication from others, without judgment, prejudice, or assumption.

    Consider these questions:

    - Someone you deeply care about routinely serenades you with a litany of complaints to the point where you tune him out. When he accuses you of not listening, what should you do?

- Do you actively listen or regularly wait for the other person to stop talking so that you can start?
- How much do you care about what others, particularly those not so close to you, have to say?

Arthur Joseph shares the following on quality communication:

> *I'm really teaching the opportunity and responsibility to the messenger, not simply the message. To create intimacy you must pay attention and practice deeper listening. I am always in the work. I am completely committed to being who I am and comfortable with that. I am committed to being with the person I'm with and communicate with them from a place of respect.*

It is imperative that you take whatever personal time you need to carefully analyze and identify your core values. This is not a task to be taken lightly and you may find that your initial list of core values changes as you challenge yourself to identify those most important to you. This journey of self-discovery, while challenging, will give you enormous freedom and will go a long way toward unlocking *the Power of You!*

CHAPTER 4

Tools to Unleash Your Power

I prefer to be true to myself, even at the hazard of incurring the ridicule of others, rather than to be false, and to incur my own abhorrence.

— *Frederick Douglass*

*W*ith new understandings come new responsibilities. We can no longer dwell in the past—especially as we seek to actualize our lives. Old issues of blame, shame, fear, or guilt must lose their grip on each aspect of today's daily life.

These familiar feelings must be replaced with a sense of contentment and happiness for which you are now 100 percent responsible. You are responsible for your expression of self and the feelings you experience. You choose to live in the present, notice more things go your way, catch good breaks, recover more readily from setbacks. You are responsible for your own happiness.

You are responsible for your environment and your circumstances. If you have sufferings, you must overcome them as no one else can or will do it for you. One hundred percent responsibility leads to the beginning of total freedom. The committee in your head belongs to you. The inner child that governs many decisions also belongs to you and must be managed. In many ways, the child must grow up.

Total accountability, rather than a heavy burden, can mean a true expression of self. One hundred percent ownership dictates that you design your world, according to your specifications. To do so, you will need new skills.

In addition to choosing core values as described in Chapter 3, this chapter will explain and show you how to implement a number of them. We will cover:

- Setting goals.
- Planning for life cycles.
- Risking self-disclosure.
- Recognizing our familiars.
- Understanding the family system.
- Holding high expectations.
- Taking personal responsibility.

Let's break them down.

Setting Goals

Setting goals has played a significant role in my life, especially early in my career. It gave me a distinct advantage over most people in their teens or twenties. Clear goals gave me a competitive edge that provided for much of the success I enjoyed. Because of this success, I felt that it was a critical tool to pass along.

First we must clearly distinguish between core values and goals. While goals are not as important as core values, they can play a key role in one's short-term pursuit of happiness, balance, and wealth. Here are some distinctions between the two.

Goals are short-term benchmarks. Core values are longterm.

Goals change regularly. Core values do not change, or do so very slowly.

Goals are always derivative and born out of core values, not the other way around.

Goals provide accountability, a feedback loop, and measurable results of one's short-term pursuits. Core values provide the foundation for the long-term pursuit of happiness, balance, and wealth.

Goals provide excitement and passion for their accomplishment along with daily or weekly feedback that tells you if you are on the right path to their accomplishment. Core values are primary drivers and the foundation for what your life is all about.

With the distinction between core values and goals firmly established, and the benefits of both close in mind, I want to review certain specific aspects of goals. I have found in my career as a businessman a prevalently low set of skills in the area of goal setting.

Goal setting accounts for at least 50 percent of the reason for my success in life. Somehow, I understood the process early on intrinsically and have concluded that once given the opportunity to distinguish between what a goal is and isn't, anyone can markedly improve her life in a short amount of time.

If you are completely unfamiliar with goal setting, don't worry. It is a skill set that most people can learn easily and with minimal effort. By the end of the next few paragraphs you will have the ability to establish goals for yourself and your life.

First, let me put forth five examples of what is typically thought of as a goal:

1. I will try to lose weight.
2. I will do everything I possibly can to grow my business next year.

48

3. I hope to make $1,000,000 next year (when last year's income was $30,000).

4. I want to live within my budget.

5. I wish I could reduce my credit card debt.

All of these are actual statements said to me by people intent on establishing a goal in an area that was important to them. These goals, while stated in a good-hearted, earnest effort, would in no way contribute to helping the person move from one step to the next. The reason the above statements did not contribute to happiness or success is they are not true goals. In order for something to be a goal it must be a SMART goal.

SMART is an acronym for the following:

S stands for specific. A goal is always stated in a simple, clear statement.

M stands for measurable. A goal is always measurable.

A stands for attainable. A goal is always attainable.

R stands for result. A goal must include a result.

T stands for trackable. A goal is always trackable.

Let's look at the previous examples of goals and rewrite them as SMART goals:

1. I will lose 10 pounds in 90 days.

2. I will increase revenues from $200,000 to $400,000 by December 31 of next year.

3. Ten years from today my annual income will be $1,000,000 a year.

4. After all my bills are paid, I will save $10 per paycheck.

5. I will reduce my credit card debt from $50,000 to $25,000 in the next six months.

Notice that all five of these goals, previously noted as hopes, tries, wishes, or wants, are now set forth as specific statements. The goal is clear and the clarity and simplicity remove virtually all opportunities for misunderstanding. Notice that all of the goals are measurable. Recognize that each goal is stated in an attainable way. There is nothing more demoralizing or demotivating to a person or a team than to set unattainable goals. The goal of a person trying to take her income from $30,000 to $1,000,000 in 12 months is unreasonable for most people. However, that same goal in 10 years would not be considered so unreasonable. Always set goals you can reach.

Next, examine the above goals and understand the significance of stating them as a result to be accomplished in a specific time frame. This brings home both the value of the goal and what must be done to accomplish the goal.

The *T* in SMART goals stands for trackable. All of these goals are trackable. You can review these goals at any time and gauge whether you are on or off course, whether you should continue with all systems go or make adjustments. All goals require adjustments along the way. The reason they need to be trackable is to make those adjustments clear and obvious.

Finally, the statement of a SMART goal is generally a beginning step in your pursuit of happiness, balance, or wealth. Once stated, other, smaller steps will be required to reach a goal. The mere desire to earn $1,000,000 a year when you presently only make $30,000, doesn't magically make it happen. There need to be a series of smaller steps or goals. Similarly, a goal to lose 10 pounds in the next 90 days would involve a series of behaviors (you would eat right, exercise, avoid empty carbohydrates, drink water, eat less sugar) to meet that goal.

The commitment to a SMART goal will create more opportunity for success because it causes you to consider what specifically must be done and what is required. Once you establish the SMART goal and begin to ask the questions, you travel along a path much more likely to yield the desired outcome.

Planning for Life Cycles

A life cycle is a planning tool that can be used to optimize your ability to create the type of sustainable change that can lead to happiness, balance, and wealth in your life.

Life cycles means that there are certain times when you have a favorable wind at your back with regard to your pursuits and other times when you more closely resemble a salmon swimming upstream. You can do it. You can get there almost by instinct and you will eventually make your way, but there are extraordinarily difficult challenges.

All of us can recall an occasion when we have been in pursuit of something extraordinarily important that came easily. The moon and stars all aligned and made it an exciting, almost easy experience. I am sure that you have also had a great idea, a great goal, that, despite its importance to you, was not meant to be—the bear stood in the stream directly in your path.

Because I grew up in a small town in Minnesota where farming was part of our lifestyle, I learned that in spring you plant the seeds for a crop to be harvested in the fall. There are certain seasons for different activities and trying to go against the current gives rise to tremendous difficulty as opposed to following naturally occurring life cycles. Like the seasons, there is a time for everything. This concept is critical in planning activities in pursuit of your happiness, balance, and wealth.

For example, in your twenties and just out of college or fresh into your work life is generally a time for great exploration and a quest to find out who you want to be when you grow up. It is a time to select a mate, pick a profession, and explore and find out how to make your way in society.

For me it was a time to see the world, to find out how to make a living that would be exciting and interesting. I wanted to visit different places. I moved from a small Minnesota town to Kingsport, Tennessee, and eventually to Los Angeles, California.

My goals were to establish myself in a business, to learn and understand what was happening in my profession. I wanted to become the best I could be as a salesman for a glass company. I modeled the best salesperson. I modeled the president of my company, the CEO of my company, and learned a great deal.

In my thirties, I got married. I wanted to get married and have children and realized that while travel was so important to me in my twenties, it was no longer as important. I had established myself in a career and been very successful. I had been promoted to vice president, to president, and then eventually purchased the company that I subsequently sold. The things I did in my thirties were much different from the things that I cared about in my twenties. I transitioned from journeyman to professional.

In my forties, my life cycle changed again. I did not want to live in a big city any longer. That was a huge shift from my twenties and thirties, where living in the big city seemed so important. In my forties, I wanted to provide a small-town atmosphere for my family where I could raise my children. I sought to continue my professional career with an emphasis on personal growth.

With this book and our company, ConsciousOne, that is what I have continued to do. The pursuit is now more of mastery, and teaching what I know. I want to educate through my experiences and tell my story so that other people can make their way along a similar path. For me, my life cycle has changed every 7 to 10 years.

In a recent interview, Arthur Joseph spoke of his own life cycles:

> *I speak about the three Ts—timing, talent, and tenacity. I assure you, tenacity is the greatest attribute, stick-to-it-ivness against all odds.*
>
> *I was in my mid-thirtys when I finally came to grips with my greatest artistic, professional, and personal challenge. Sociologists were simply wrong when they said that the fear of public speaking is the greatest fear. The greatest fear I discovered was ownership of our power and fear of abandonment. This ownership of power and not being afraid of what somebody else thinks of you while you're being who you are, is a huge piece of my life's work.*

When you look back on your career or your experiences what are your life cycles? How often do things seem to fundamentally change? It is important to look at and understand your life cycles because it allows you to predict when possible changes are going to come next.

I graduated from high school in 1980. That was a critical-change year for me. Then 1990 was the year I sold my first business and cashed my first seven-figure check at the age of 29. The year 2000 marked a big change for me as well.

I have noticed that while every 10 years seems to be a life cycle for me, every five years brings a smaller change. Now I pay close attention when coming up on years that end with the number zero or the number five. When you look at your life, when did the big events happen? Does your life change every 2, 5, 10, 15 years? Can you recognize a life cycle?

It's interesting to note that levels of knowledge often coincide with life cycles. You begin as an apprentice without much experience, perhaps not even much knowledge. You just have a desire and a lot of energy. From there you move to journeyman, still with a tremendous amount of energy and the desire to practice your profession or craft—and a little bit of experience. You probably have been taught or had a mentor help you along the way. Then comes the level of professional—you have practiced your craft for many years and take great pride in its exercise. The last level is that of master. This is where you have advanced beyond professional and now give back to your craft, trade, or career. You are now a teacher and perhaps act as a mentor or coach. This is the highest level of practice in any profession.

The key planning tool in terms of a life cycle is to understand that no one moves from apprentice directly to professional, nor from journeyman to master. Each steps takes time, and there is no getting around it.

As Sonia Choquette so aptly explained in an interview:

There's a learning curve and nobody can get past it. Many people don't succeed because they don't want to enter that learning curve of student, apprentice, journeyman, master.

You have to be willing to be a beginner. You have to go through the process of learning by doing. You can't be instantly at the top of your game.

A guy I was working with once said to me: "It's easy for you to say, you're a published writer."

I replied: "Do you know the first time I wrote a book? I was asked if English was my first language."

I had a choice then. I was humiliated, but what, just quit? I certainly had plenty of encouragement to do so. I was willing to be embarrassed and get past that and learn how to do it better. We have to get past our fear of embarrassment. Perseverance, tenacity and courage are important feelings to have. I honestly have never seen anybody succeed without courage. I call it fire in the belly.

As you use life cycles for planning, you know that with each endeavor there is a period of time when you are going to be the apprentice. You will develop certain skills to become the journeyman, other skills to become the professional, and finally those needed to be a master.

Risking Self-Disclosure

When you understand your core values and take the risk of declaring them, a unique challenge awaits you, one that will give you much feedback—some positive, some negative. Once you strongly state who you are, others will do whatever they can to force you to conform to their vision of you—particularly if you have had a long relationship with them, such as is the case with family members.

With the knowledge that the feedback from your self-disclosure will be both positive and negative, it's important to plan for that and explore what those discussions may look like ahead of time. Role-play the dialogue in your head and prepare yourself for potential outcomes. "Gosh, I've just realized that personal growth is very important to me—Dad, Wife, Husband." Talk it out internally. Anticipate the responses and decide how you want to react in each instance.

For some of us, defining our values may feel liberating and transformational—a declarative statement that brings happiness and contentment. We may feel the desire to act as the town crier and share our values with the world.

For most, disclosing who we are is a terrifying proposition. We need tools to get started. One way to address your initial trepidation is to ask yourself the question: "If I risk five percent more self-disclosure . . . ?"

Leave an open-ended space for the responses to flow. The answers might include:

"I'll get more clarity about myself."

"I'm going to be happier."

"I'll let people know who I really am."

"People will get to know the real me."

"I wonder what people will think."

"I wonder if people will still like me."

"My parents will tell me to be quiet."

Notice that the process of self-disclosure begins with us to ourselves first and then to others.

Dr. Nathaniel Branden offered this point of view in an interview:

Before there can be self-disclosure with regard to others, the process begins with my willingness to know what I myself am feeling. Am I willing to look at and be honest about my feelings? That precedes the whole issue of self-disclosure.

If we are trying to help people be more self-disclosing, without first helping them to become more self-aware and willing to look at their internal world and what they're feeling in different contexts, we will fail. If we help people and treat them with respect in their struggles to articulate their feelings, then we can support self-disclosure. People can be fearful. They feel others will think badly of them if they talk about the time they were afraid. People's fear of disapproval or mockery is often the great paralyzer when it comes to being self-disclosing. Perhaps the saddest, most preposterous thing in my whole career as a psychotherapist came when I heard a client say, in therapy, that he had never said to his wife in 40 years of marriage: "I love you." And I said, "Why not?" And he answered: "She'd lose all respect for me." That's the reductio ad absurdum of the terror of self-disclosure. The poor soul feels, in admitting he has this strong feeling, that she won't see him as manly any more. That's a tragic extreme example.

What it dramatizes and makes clear is that the issue of disclosing who I am to you comes after I look at disclosing it to myself.

Once we share with others what our values are, we begin to connect with them on a deep, emotional level. Some respond well. Especially as you become comfortable, some will embrace your self-disclosure. Others will psychologically run away from you.

This book is about *the Power of You*—not the power your parents or spouse have over you. You want to improve your life. In order for that to happen, you have to practice self-awareness and risk sharing with others what you are truly about. This doesn't require setting aside time during which you plan to consciously connect. That would imply trying to force others onto your schedule. This is about your personal responsibility to risk self-disclosure about who you are on an ongoing basis.

If you feel badly or blue, you can share that:

"I'm feeling poorly because my dog died."

"I'm feeling uncomfortable and nervous because my partner has been diagnosed with cancer."

"I'm disappointed with the way this has been handled."

The opposite also applies:

"I'm really excited about what we're doing together."

"I love this type of work and could not be happier doing it."

"I am elated when I see these kind of results."

The use of *feeling* words is an important component of self-disclosure, of connecting with people. However, do not be surprised when most people fail to respond in a meaningful way. You're not doing it for them. You're doing it because it's important to you.

It is a wonderful experience when you attract into your life those that mirror your ability to self-disclose, connect with you, and share how they feel. You will pull those in as you risk your own self-disclosure. Self-disclosure is about making yourself visible in the world, making yourself present—allowing people to see you for who you are and what you are.

Most of us have one or two people in our lives that we immediately connect with no matter how long it has been since we've seen them or what has happened in our life. In a matter of minutes we drop into a deep emotional connection without any need to talk about the weather or peripheral stuff. We talk about important matters in our lives and how we feel about them.

Actually, that's what we need to do with everyone—with the understanding that not everybody will reciprocate, and in fact, most won't. Those who do respond in kind, who risk self-disclosure without a lot of drama, explanation, or justification, we identify as people whom we want to invest more in—kindred souls.

You'll decide that you can do more of that with them as you move forward. You'll disclose more of your personal values, seek to discover how many of them are similar—and will usually find that to be so.

When you risk self-disclosure, you are being who you are and giving others the opportunity to reciprocate in kind to identify themselves and who they are. As you go through this, you will find few, not many, who want to take the risk. It's important to manage your expectations. Expect to be pleasantly and wonderfully surprised when someone does respond in kind and do not be disappointed when someone doesn't.

If it happens seldom, chances are that you are not surrounded with people who share your core values. In order to find happiness, balance, and wealth, that will need to change. Without reciprocation of self-disclosure, it will be much more difficult for you to find contentment and peace within yourself. You may need to shift your relationships to those who share similar core values, especially to create happiness. If you don't, that's your responsibility. Others will not change because you want them to.

You have *the Power of You!* to find the right relationships. Once you start down the path, *you* more than ever need to take charge and make the challenging choices about who adds to your life, who shares the values and who doesn't. The choice is always yours.

Beware of patterns of sabotage. The way many people operate is to seldom disclose anything and engage in a dangerous cycle: harbor, not disclose, harbor, build up tremendous amounts of junk and then spew or dump all over someone else. Not only can this create pain and angst—it is ineffective in leading a balanced life.

You can't operate like the camel that heaps one more straw on the back only to create a huge toxic dump once the back breaks. This happens far too regularly—at offices, in families, with people who we believe to be important to us.

We have to choose people based on shared core values—choose to self-disclose and connect regularly. This is not to be confused with lack of conflict. There will always be conflict. The difference is that with shared core values, conflict facilitates itself in a positive, productive way. We gain insight into ourselves through considering a different point of view from someone who we know views the world much like we do.

However, conflict with people of differing core values tends to be debilitating and deflating. Consider a relationship with someone of differing core values. Conflict leads to a blowup due to lack of ongoing connecting and resolving of differences. This is completely the opposite of conflict with people of similar core values. This type of conflict will be based on feedback and accountability to core values—things that are very valuable to your growth.

Use simple feeling statements. You don't need 50 words to say something. You push people away and don't risk self-disclosure when you take that long to express yourself.

Simple brings people closer.

Complex pushes people away.

Simple creates intimacy.

Complex leads to distance.

A simple declarative statement brings an ability to connect at a deep level quickly. Here are a few examples:

Positive

"I feel happy that you're in my life."

"I love you."

"This feels important."

"I feel happy."

"I'm glad."

"I'm happy."

"I'm excited."

"This feels good."

Negative

"This feels bad."

"I'm angry."

"I'm disappointed."

"I'm hurt."

"I'm sad."

"I'm blue."

"I'm mad."

These kinds of words do not require much elaboration or explanation. They only require that you say them without prologue or epilogue.

This is how we connect without drama.

We reveal ourselves quickly.

We share who we are and how we truly feel.

Whether or not the other person responds is secondary. The important issue is that you disclose yourself.

Once we begin to self-disclose and share how we feel in a given moment, we may have the tendency to expect people to reciprocate—we may want them to. Our expectation in that regard will not always be met. We must stay with the process anyway for our own sake—*the Power of You!* does not depend on reciprocation. It is not likely that those people who have surrounded you until this point are going to respond in kind once you begin to exercise the self-disclosure muscle. If you try to teach and convince those around you to do what you're doing, you set yourself up for disappointment. Whether they do or don't is up to them.

Notice that as a child, you had a strong self-disclosure skill set. When you came home from school and Mom asked you how you felt, you answered "I'm sad," without knowing why. It was just how you felt. You may have gotten a response along the lines of: "No, you're not. How can you be sad with all that you have? When I was a kid . . ." or "Don't be sad. Put on a happy face . . ."

Our models for understanding how we feel and experience the world came from teachers (our parents) who did not understand these models all that well. They did not acknowledge the feeling states and the importance of them. The honesty of the feeling was not considered as important as "boosting" the child up.

What behavior is learned by the child through this type of interaction? When a mother denies the child's feeling and admonishes the child to not feel a certain way, the child assumes that he or she was wrong to feel sad. The child makes the assumption that he or she is wrong, because in the child's mind there is no way that the parents could be wrong.

Consider that this happened over and over in our youth—thousands of missed opportunities to connect. It is no wonder that we feel disconnected and shut down from who we are and what we are truly about. These early roadmaps create confusion that we need to sort through as adults.

If we work with the common major feelings—happy, sad, angry, excited, glad, hurt, and so on—and ask a given person if he relates to any of these or if he feels a lot of distance from any of them, we usually find that one or more is close, and one or more is distant. We associate closely with one and disconnect from another.

This exercise can point us in the direction of understanding our roadmap. If as a child we were repeatedly told that we did not feel sad even though we did, that creates a familiar that stays with us until we address it—and so on. If our gerbil died, we might naturally feel sad for a few days. This natural feeling may be tough to hold onto with mother constantly arguing that we didn't or shouldn't feel that way.

If we were always bubbling with energy, smiling, loud, and so on but came from a family that held expressing emotion as a bad thing for whatever reason—faith, religion, post–Depression era—this enthusiasm may have been suppressed.

Do any of these sound familiar?

"Go to your room."

"You're too loud."

"Pipe down."

"Children are to be seen but not heard."

Your family may literally have killed the excitement and energy in your life—the very things that your life deserves.

If you came from a family that never expressed anger or conflict, how could you know how to address a situation where conflicting values arise? What if no one ever raised their voice in your house? Or what if you came from a high-conflict environment where everyone yells and screams? If so, you may never feel loved without conflict.

Assumptions contribute to our roadmaps and shape the way we are. Those patterns may have worked in childhood, yet have no bearing today. They need to be revealed, addressed, and transformed or discarded.

Recognizing Our Familiars

Familiars are feeling states learned at an early age that create an imprint on us that continues in adult life and govern us—with or without our knowledge, with or without our approval. For example, a person who grew up in a high-conflict world will seek out a high-conflict environment in which to attempt to flourish, since that is what he knows—the stereotypical yelling and gesturing Italian family from a movie or television show. That setting becomes that person's familiar—it feels comfortable. That person may only feel attracted to a high-drama individual—and vice versa.

If you are reading this and did not come from that type of background, you may think: "That's crazy—why would someone do that?" And yet it happens all the time. Alternatively, if you come from a low-conflict environment, you may never feel attracted to or may even feel repulsed by a high-conflict person.

These illogical feelings stem from our familiars. To create sustainable change, we need to understand this phenomenon, be aware of it, and address it—especially if we want to create happiness, balance, and wealth. If we understand our familiars, we understand that we have a strong desire to recreate them. With this understanding, we then have the ability to choose that same roadmap or to change it and create something new—one that allows for personal transformation. Without awareness, we have no choice. In the end, the only reason to recreate a familiar is if it serves us. If not, we don't have to.

Arleah Shechtman defines familiars as follows:

The familiar is an emotional state that we dealt with as a child when we learned how to cope. We build all kinds of coping mechanisms and ways of dealing with whatever that emotional state was. As a grown-up we tend to seek out situations where that familiar feeling is close at hand. If it's not, we will re-create it. It's important because it's safe. What makes it safe is that we know how to deal with it. We know how to deal with feeling bad all the time, because that's how we grew up. We grew up feeling something all the time and because we felt that, we developed this whole complex of defenses and reactions that we know how to cope with. Stepping out of your familiar means you have to develop new coping mechanisms, new ways of dealing with life. As time goes on, when you get triggered into those old places, that's a signal to look at what just happened. Once you trigger an old place that means that someone has done something to trigger you, or something has happened that you need to attend to. That then becomes something that you can use to your benefit to help you rather than take you down.

It is important to note that familiars that served us as children may not serve us at all as adults. They may not be good for us in any way. Consider once again the child who grew up in a high-conflict, high-argument environment, where everyone expressed themselves by yelling and arguing. For that child, the only way to gain any visibility in the family and feel loved was to do what they experienced in their environment, to scream and yell. That feeling state of anger and conflict that the child grew up with is what she or he will attempt to recreate later in life when seeking love or happiness with a mate. The anger and confusion will be repeatedly recreated.

Notice that the vociferous arguing, whether we agree with it or not, did in fact work for the child at one time. By following the family pattern, the child was able to "be seen" and feel loved. Without awareness, that same pattern will continue all through adulthood. However, if we know of its existence, we can make a choice. "I continue this pattern of being loud and boisterous throughout my life because it is me . . ." *or* "I choose to understand this pattern as a feeling state created as a young child as a result of growing up in that environment." I can then decide if that is an appropriate expression of love for me as an adult or whether I want to consciously bring out that familiar, examine it for what it is, and make a different choice. Most importantly, I can allow the sad feeling over unmet needs to be acknowledged, mourned and grieved.

Arleah Shechtman further states:

We all come out of our families with gifts and wounds. We keep the gifts and hopefully heal from the wounds. Sometimes the wounds are hard to understand or see. The most grievous thing that can happen to a child is nothing. In some ways, I wish sometimes that my dad had hit me with a stick, because then I could say, I hurt right here in this spot because you hit me. Its hard to explain why I hurt when there's nothing happening to me. The important thing is what conclusion a child draws at the time of that abandonment and what decision they make about whatever conclusion they drew. That then becomes the driving force still true now. The decisions that we make at three and seven and twelve and all in between are as operational today as they were they day you made them. The process of healing is to help make a new decision.

The imprint of the familiar is enormous, regardless of how inappropriate it may seem. A familiar keeps us safe and hidden, away from something we perceive as able to harm us if we express our need in the moment. It takes mourning and grieving the loss of the mistreatment experienced as a child to fully overcome it.

A powerful familiar can take us all the way to a place of not even being able to feel attracted to people who treat us well, if we came from a place of continuous abuse. Consider a childhood where expectations were continuously quashed in many ways. Without awareness, we replay that imprint over and over:

"You don't deserve any more than . . ."

"How dare you ask for . . ."

"You'd better shut up and not ask for what you want . . ."

With an understanding of the familiar, the adult needs to go back and grieve and mourn the loss, such that it can be let go of and new models adopted—a worthiness to deserve, a greater sense of self-worth, and so on.

Understanding the Family System

All of us grew up with and are presently involved in some family system—an organization that has its own identity—the Smith family, the Jones family. In each one there is an order or a hierarchy much like the cast of a play—the Dad role, the Mom role, the sibling role, the child role and so on.

Think about the family you grew up in and the one that you are in now. There are lead actors, bit players, and a supporting cast. Everyone has a role to play and all actors use each others' roles, including yours, to identify their own. By definition, this means that everyone is vested in maintaining the status quo, in making sure that each actor plays his or her assigned role.

For example, if you are the good daughter, there are many family members invested in that role of you as the "good daughter." If you are the "bad daughter," the same applies. The family has made an emotional investment in that role and wants to make sure that you don't change it.

The son who finishes law school suddenly declares that he doesn't want to enter Dad's legal practice but would rather move to Alaska and write about fishing. How does the family system conspire to keep the good son in his proper role? Are they likely to support that decision? What does the family system do to that self-disclosure from "the good son"?

The party-girl daughter uncharacteristically reveals her passion to become a doctor and help people with rare forms of cancer. How does the family system help her or hurt her? Is the family system going to allow or adjust to her self-disclosure?

A system is defined by a set of processes and rules that allow that system to work. When each person plays his role, the system operates as defined. In discovering *the Power of You!*, you may find that your declared values have nothing to do with the role you play or have historically played in the family system. In fact, that role may be the opposite of your newly declared you. Most family systems will resist change, at least in the beginning, because the family system works only if everyone remains in the roles they were assigned early in life. Otherwise, the established family system will break down. To buck the system, courage is required—the ability to persevere.

To even begin the process we need to understand our own family system. Ask yourself the following questions:

Are you aware that a family system exists?

Are you aware of your role in it?

Are you comfortable in that role?

Is that role contributing to happiness, balance, and wealth?

Think about a family reunion during the holidays. On such an occasion many of us will revert to our historic role—especially because if we don't, it will threaten everyone else's enjoyment of the holiday.

This role may have little or nothing to do with who you are or want to become today, especially with an awareness of your core values. What do you do? Do you challenge the system and cause a potential uproar or play the role assigned to you—justify that since it is only for a few days, you don't want to upset the other members of the family?

We've grown up with the concept of spending a lot of time together and the notion that this is a way to get to know each other well. If we go on vacation for a week together "we really get to connect" Most of us believe that time spent together equals deeper knowledge of those family members.

Others have had a slightly different experience. By the second day with their family, they are already uncomfortable and ready to leave. We need to remove this paradigm that time spent equals deep knowing of a person. It is an old myth that no longer applies—if it ever did. Again the key is to become aware of your role and take the time to analyze the aspects of it that serve you and those that don't, the aspects that align with your core values and those that don't.

Heroes surround us—those who risk self-disclosure and declare their core values—those who challenge the family system and their assigned roles. Heroism involves the statement, "I am going to be the person that I decide and declare to be." Heroism involves the inner frontier. The western frontier involved staking a claim and defending it. The inner frontier involves staking a claim about *you* and defending it, only this time, the stakes are even higher—they're all about you—your happiness, balance, and wealth.

Holding High Expectations

As part of his extensive writings, Dr. Nathaniel Branden included the following quote:

> *The level of our self-esteem creates a set of implicit expectations about what is possible and appropriate to us. These ex-*

pectations engender the actions that turn them into realities. And the realities then confirm and strengthen the original beliefs. Self-esteem, high or low, is the generator of self-fulfilling prophecies.

In this new era, one of the ways that we show that we care about others and want them to succeed is by holding high expectations of those around us. This means that when someone commits to getting something done at work or completing a project at home, you hold the expectation that they will come through. In addition, it means that you are capable of letting them know how you feel when they *either* complete the project *or* miss the commitment.

Previously we might have ignored a failed commitment, granted extra time, accepted excuses, or mitigated the issue in some fashion. In other words, we allowed a person to fail to meet an agreed-upon obligation. "It's okay that you missed this one as long as you make the next commitment." This type of compromised agreement bleeds into relationships with spouse and others. In today's world, holding high expectations of others requires us not to be co-dependent or enabling. We cannot be caretakers of those around us.

An extreme example often honored in our society is the selfless mother who takes care of her children by completing tasks that the children are both capable of and have agreed to do for themselves—cleaning their room, brushing their teeth, getting their homework done. Or we might allow a spouse to spend money beyond an agreed budget. Or we might choose to do our mate's tasks and then resent them for what they did not do—the classic "tit for tat."

Failure to hold high expectations can also manifest in more subtle ways:

We can selfishly decide that we are too tired to connect.

We might fail to acknowledge the impact of a family member's substance abuse.

We might reward activity instead of productivity at work.

The way in which we hold people accountable is by expressing our feelings when expectations have not been met. Simple phrases can let us share a feeling and let others know how we experienced their missing a commitment:

"Mary, I felt disappointed when the budget you promised for Tuesday was not done on time."

"Mom, I felt hurt when you missed my dance recital."

"Jerry, I felt sad and scared when you spent more than we had agreed."

There are two components to this. One is the ability to express our feelings to the other person and disclose how we feel—an acknowledgment to ourselves. Equally important is that the other person hears us say it and is held accountable by our expression. If we hold identical or similar core values, the expression of disappointment, sadness, fear, or hurt from an important person in our life to us should give us great pause—not just a flashing yellow signal but a big red siren going off.

In most family, work, or personal interactions we get into situations where we are required to interface with others and make commitments on an ongoing basis:

"I'll pick you up at eight."

"I'll see you for dinner tonight."

"I'll be there at four-thirty."

"I'll send that file later today."

"That project will be done next week Thursday."

"We can make this happen."

"The deal will close on Wednesday."

"I'll meet you at the mall at five P.M."

When we don't hold someone accountable for delivering what is promised, it is a form of abandonment, a form of expressing how we don't care. It ignores what someone else has expressed is important. Holding someone accountable for what she said she would do is a loving, caring act, one that hears the other person and what she stated was important to her.

When our children say they will clean their room each day and they don't, if we don't bring the issue up, we do neither them nor ourselves any favors. We hurt both sides.

Dr. Branden, in a recent interview, clarified the need for all of us to help those we care about by believing in them and holding a high expectation of them:

Some people don't have the inner sense that a major level of success, happiness, or love is possible or appropriate for them. Somehow that's not their story, not their fate. They struggle against the feelings that get in the way of people giving their best to whatever it is they're involved in, whether it be a relationship or a business. It's like trying to fight against a gravitational pull. They strain to go up while the gravitational pull drags them down. The gravitational pull is all the negative self-concepts that get in the way of self-ac- tualizing, in the way of fulfillment, and in the way of love or happiness or wealth. That is why I've written somewhere that self-concept is destiny.

Automobile maker Henry Ford, whom we don't think of as a psychologist, once said something very interesting: "If you think you can do something or if you think you can't, you're right."

We must make sure that we use our judgment to understand what is more important. Should we ignore, abandon, and choose not to acknowledge that people important to us are not living up to their commitments by remaining quiet and not expressing our feelings? *Or* should we share with people how important they are to us by letting them know that the missing of their commitments and obligations impacted us deeply? Holding high expectations means honoring those around us by expressing both our elation and our disappointment about the commitments that we make and those made to us.

Taking Personal Responsibility

Personal responsibility comes from the understanding that we blame no one else for where we are in life, where we have been, or where we are headed. Where we are today is a perfect manifestation of the skill sets that we have used up until this point. It is not about blaming our parents, our teachers, our spouse, our boss, our partners, our politicians, or anyone else.

All of us at one point or another have succumbed to the blame game. Think about the way you attribute the traits you may have received from others that you are not particularly pleased with:

"I'm hot tempered because my mother was Irish."

"We always yelled in our family—that's why I yell."

"We argued in our family—that's how you proved you were smart."

"We never raised our voices—we were always polite."

Terminal uniqueness is another huge roadblock to creating sustainable change:

"I am so different that I can't be helped."

"I separate myself from an effective solution to my afflictions—because I'm so unique."

"I can see how that might work for so-and-so but it certainly can't work for me."

"That doesn't work for me because I was raised poor."

"That doesn't work for me because I was raised rich."

"I can't do that because my dad was an alcoholic" (or fill in the reason—read "excuse"—why I can't be helped).

Interestingly, while we may tend to blame our difficult traits on someone else, when it comes to our positive skill sets, somehow we find a way to take credit for their full development. What a dichotomy. In terms of our ability to create sustainable change, we must understand that we are 100 percent responsible for both the negative and the positive. We are 100 percent responsible for using the positive skills, as well as using the challenging traits, weaknesses, and so on in a positive, value-creating way.

It goes without saying that when we use our traits in a negative way we are 100 percent responsible for the consequences of that behavior as well. The key to growth is to understand how personal responsibility impacts your ability to create sustainable change. If you only take responsibility for your good traits, you're only going to have short-term growth that will be followed by reversion to familiars. If you take responsibility for your challenging traits and weaknesses and other assumptions made that no longer serve as an adult, own them and understand them, they release their power over you. If we don't take personal responsibility for challenges, we can never create sustainable change. Any major advancement we make will pull us so far out of our comfort zone that we will self-sabotage or revert back to behavior that somehow pulls us back into an old familiar, a place where we feel safe, a place that we know. Our forward motion will soon be met with a backward slide. We might choose to:

Pick a fight with a spouse.

Screw up a business venture.

Overeat.

Indulge in substance abuse.

Find a way to allow some other familiar to rear its ugly head.

We must take 100 percent responsibility for all of our traits, understand them and recognize them when they creep in and impact us. It's great to acknowledge and recognize the positives. That has much value. However, we need to work on the negatives, understand them, and release their power over us. The point is to not ignore any of them—especially when it comes to attaining balance.

One quick note—there is a school of thought in business that suggests that we need to "understand our strengths" and "seek to develop our weaknesses into strengths" or at best make them neutral. For example, if your interpersonal skills are lacking, that's where you should focus to bring them up to par.

Those who embrace these behavior-assessment tools tend to spend much time working on weaknesses as opposed to capitalizing on strengths. Ultimately this proves ineffective. Being aware of challenges and weaknesses and taking personal responsibility for them does not mean spending our lives turning them into positive traits. It means being aware of them and how they can sabotage what we might want to accomplish. A focus on strengths can yield big results. The key is to also understand our weaknesses and how they creep in to sabotage us without clear awareness on our part.

All of these new skills and tools can help us create true sustainable change. Even though they may not feel natural when we first begin to experiment with them, the good news is that their use will improve our lives immediately. Beginning that process is a positive, powerful step in manifesting *the Power of You!*

CHAPTER 5

The Power of
the Conscious Triangle

To me, there are three things we all should do every day.
We should do this every day of our lives. Number one is
laugh. You should laugh every day. Number two is think.
You should spend some time in thought. And number
three is, you should have your emotions moved to tears,
could be happiness or joy. But think about it. If you laugh,
you think, and you cry, that's a full day. That's a heck of a
day. You do that seven days a week, you're going to have
something special.

—Jim Valvano

The Conscious Triangle offers us an evolved model for the new world exposed in the first four chapters of this book. As you may recall, *conscious* means to be aware not only of our surroundings, but of ourselves at all levels. Let's review the basic evolution of consciousness for most people bearing in mind that throughout our lives we go through different levels of awareness.

The first level of awareness is one of stimulus response, the most primitive mode of relating to the world.

As a child, stimulus response goes something like this:

I am hungry—I cry.

I am hurt—I scream.

I am happy—I jump up and down.

While basic, this level of consciousness is straightforward and clear. All of us have experienced and seen examples of infants and young children in the stimulus response mode.

In our teens, our mode of relating to the world becomes increasingly murky. Our awareness centers on how the world revolves around us and how stupid everyone else is in comparison, especially our parents and other adults. In actuality, this level of awareness is not far beyond stimulus response.

In expressing displeasure toward others, what we generally convey is that our needs are not being met. Much like the baby or the infant, unmet needs trigger an emotional response, in this case a lashing out. Many teenagers have the ability to communicate their displeasure with great ease.

"Everyone in the world is so stupid besides me."

"My parents are such buffoons, idiots, bozos."

"They never listen to anything I say."

"Why is everyone so mean to me?"

What this really reflects is a teenager's inability to communicate needs in a way that can be met and a lack of awareness of what these needs are in the first place. Notice that undefined core values keep what is important completely vague. In addition to this lack of awareness is the inability of the teenager to communicate feelings. It goes without saying that this does not breed a great environment for being conscious.

As we move into our twenties, we are thrust into a more independent space. We must fend for ourselves and become aware of our financial responsibility to subsist and pay bills. The biological desire to seek out a mate follows the natural order of human beings. Notice once again that this mode of relating has progressed slightly further beyond stimulus response but not much.

Here are some typical thoughts and statements of our twenties:

"I need rent money."

"I need money to pay the bills."

"I need money to go out."

"I need money to live my life."

"Why can't I find the right person?"

"Where have all the good men/women gone?"

From a financial perspective, only after the fiftieth or one-hundredth paycheck does a deeper, more important question arise:

"Is this all there is?"

"Is this all that I will be doing for the next few decades?"

From a relationship perspective, the second or third failed relationship gives rise to doubt and begins to trigger a new line of thinking:

"Maybe I'll just settle down with this person."

"Relationships are not all that they are cracked up to be."

"Maybe relationships aren't for me."

"Men/women suck."

Both with finances and relationships, the initial phase of questioning more often than not begins from a negative perspective: "Is this all there is?" For many, the sad answer is: "Yes." They then spend the rest of their life complaining and whining.

Those who seek a little more deeply answer otherwise: "No—there must be more."

An inner questioning begins:

"What more do I want?"

"What is important to me?"

"What is missing in my life?"

The probing process continues from "what" to "how":

"How do I find what is missing?"

"How am I to understand other people?"

"How do I understand myself?"

The easy "if I just had more money, everything would be perfect" response falls short, though initially many of us might go there.

Consciousness and awareness must include both the things we are happy about and want to include in our lives as well as those we want to remove, address, and understand. This is especially important to recognize because it is far easier to move toward something that we want than it is to remove something that we do not.

Consider questions that stir up the process of self-discovery. Consciousness includes who you are when no one else is around. In the quest to create sustainable change, happiness, balance, and wealth, you must peel back the surface and reveal the aspects of yourself that work as well as the challenges that hold you back or bring you down.

Your discovery process may be helped by these questions:

What are your strongest traits, things you are most proud of?

What are your biggest weaknesses or challenges?

What are the three greatest contributors to your happiness?

What are the three greatest contributors to establishing balance in your life?

What are the three greatest contributors to creating wealth for yourself?

What are the three biggest roadblocks to your daily happiness?

What are the three biggest roadblocks to establishing balance in your life?

What are the three biggest roadblocks to creating wealth in your life?

What did you learn from your mother that contributes positively to the above?

What did you learn from your mother that creates a roadblock to the above?

What did you learn from your father that contributes positively to the above?

What did you learn from your father that creates a roadblock to the above?

How does the family you grew up with contribute to your life today?

How does the family you grew up with create a roadblock?

How does your present family contribute?

How does your present family hold you back?

Notice that these questions are outwardly directed, focused on the influence of others. They will help you in the process of raising your own consciousness. These starter questions will in turn lead to more inwardly directed, deeper questions later in the book.

One of the ways of raising consciousness is to have a self-assessment tool, one that helps you understand who you are, where you stand in relation to others in the world, and how you relate to them. The *Conscious Triangle* provides such a tool. The power of the Conscious Triangle breaks down each individual's primary actions into three components like three legs of a stool, each one required for the stool to stand. To maximize the power of the Conscious Triangle, all three must work together.

We all have *feelings, thoughts,* and *actions.* Our internal frontier is always processed through one or more of these three areas. When any of the three is neglected, this is generally to our detriment. Happiness, balance, and wealth and sustainable change can occur only when you integrate all three components. Let's examine each leg of the Conscious Triangle in order to help you identify which is your dominant trait.

The first component is labeled the *Doer.* The Doer is the action-oriented person, always busy, always performing some task. A typical response to the question "How are you?" will garner a laundry list of what they are doing, not how they are feeling. They are generally high-energy people, moving around at a fast pace in comparison to others.

They have a bias toward action, a positive trait when it comes to accomplishing things. The great value of a Doer is his or her ability to take action and get things done. This skill cannot be overstated. Even though this same skill can act as an impediment when it comes to connecting with a feeling or a thought, at the end of the day, action is necessary.

Dr. Nathaniel Branden, added this thought about taking action:

> *Say you have somebody who has a business and it's not anywhere near what the owner feels it could be. Then you have to*

immediately look at what could you do that would allow you to be more successful than you are now? Are there things that you could be doing that would cause your business to grow, but you're not doing them? That question is almost always answered with a sheepish "yes." Then we have to look at why. If you know that these things would be beneficial and could bring you closer to where you want to be, what's the obstacle? What strategies can we develop to overcome that obstacle? What needs to be done?

The second component is the *Feeler*, sometimes called the *Artist*. This is the person who processes all activities and reactions around him through how he feels. When asked the same question, "How are you?" they might answer: "I feel sad," or "I feel happy." The answer will include words like *excited, sad, blue, disappointed*, and so on—"feeling words."

Feelers process everything that goes on around them through their feeling state. This is a positive trait for connecting with others and being able to empathize, understand, relate, or communicate a feeling as the impetus to stay connected through feelings is high. The desire of the Feeler to take action or to logically process thoughts is lower. This tendency to process everything through feelings can act as an impediment when taking action or making decisions.

One of the challenges of the Feeler is that many of us have been shut down at an early age. Dr. Branden shares this point of view:

When we were young, nobody told us that our wants mattered. We often got the opposite message. A lot of people feel: Who am I to want? Who am I to dream? That's the enemy of high achievement because it's the enemy of high expectation.

Here again, we deal with a self-esteem problem and a self-concept problem.

People have to feel entitled to be great, entitled to love and be loved, entitled to be happy, providing they will do what's needed to achieve these values. It isn't that life owes us, we have to do something, but you need the inner conviction that anything that I can earn, I deserve.

The third component is the *Thinker*. This is the rational individual who processes much of his or her experience through the intellect and intelligence. This trait proves most valuable in evaluating whether a plan or idea is rational and makes logical sense. The Thinker's strength is in his or her use of reason, logic, and rationale; this is the ideal person to craft and analyze a business plan. However, you would not look to a Thinker for passion or excitement. In addition, the Thinker may have difficulty tapping into the energy of action.

We can never turn off the Thinker. To quote Dr. Branden:

Without the guidance of our intelligence and our rational intellect, we are very, very limited. This may have been passive since very early in life. A person may have been put down so many times early in life that they wonder what's the use? They may be lazy. What we know for a certainty is that if we don't use our intelligence, searching out everything that could be relevant, that could help us achieve our goals, then to sit and daydream about them, accomplishes nothing.

Our mind needs to be hungry for information, feedback, mentoring, reading, studying—anything that will give us more to help us move toward the achievement of our own aspirations. Without an active mind, a mind hungry for knowledge, life is going to be disappointing.

People who don't think but spend a great deal of time pre-occupied with their feelings, are not really that conscious about their feelings either. They're not dealing with the anxiety they feel. They're not encountering the anger and the bitterness, the resentment that they feel, the defiance that they feel. People can wallow on one or two feelings or emotions, hurts or resentments without having any real intelligence about their emotional life whatsoever. You need to think clearly, to be clear-headed about your feelings and emotions.

The power of the Conscious Triangle is when we *put all three of these traits to work for us at the same time.* The true power of the conscious triangle comes from the simultaneous integration of all three components.

Be cautious not to overly label yourself. While all of us have a dominant trait, we each possess all three components of the Conscious Triangle within us. The key to happiness, balance, and wealth lies in integrating them all, with a full understanding that our dominant trait will always be more developed than the others.

To tap into *the Power of You!*, we must train ourselves to process our daily life through all three components. For example, a Doer entrepreneur or self-made businessperson, constantly busy with producing for his business, might never take time for himself, his family, or other activities outside the context of his business. While many laud producers and praise their achievements, there are times when productivity without clarity on feelings and thoughts or core values can produce unhappiness—an out-of-balance lifestyle that ultimately may even sabotage financial success.

Productivity or industriousness without an understanding of the underlying core values, without reason or rationality, without inspiration or a feeling of happiness, is only slightly different than working the chain gang. The slight difference is that instead of a prison you sleep in your own bed at night.

This exaggerated example uses a businessperson whom most of us identify as a stereotype. However, it applies just as readily to a mother whose productivity is vested in the activities of home or children, while her hopes and dreams lie outside. We all know of parents, especially mothers, who are busy toting kids from event to event. The business of these activities is the same as the productivity of the entrepreneur, done under the banner of self-sacrifice, what parents should do, regardless of whether the activities follow core values. One is too busy to notice how much things hurt.

No one doubts the value of being a great parent and the efforts required. The point is not "good parenting," but rather the escapism that can accompany the endless tasks that a parent becomes immersed in—laundry, taxi service, cleaning, homework, and so on—all consuming tasks that bury core values under the banner of "sacrifice."

Doers are afraid to admit that they are not working on matters of true importance to them—so they just stay busy. They refuse to allow time for questions, contemplation, or self-reflection.

Thinkers process activities through the intellect in a rational, reasonable, logical fashion. They analyze and predict outcomes of a given situation without much regard to any feelings. Thinkers have the ability to make decisions after digesting myriad data and can forecast likely results. They make good plans of action. The value of the ability to utilize reason, logic, and rational thought cannot be overstated.

However, the ability to reason and deduce can cause paralysis by analysis where the energy and excitement of an idea or endeavor can be drained out by a Thinker. If you ask a Thinker, "How are you?" you will likely get a perfunctory "Fine." You will not hear a feeling word such as *happy* or *sad*, though occasionally you may get a long-winded explanation of what is going on in his life without emotional context. In extreme cases, Thinkers can be perceived as dead in their outlook, not filled with much life. Do not let this outward appearance fool you. It is simply the manifestation of an overdeveloped thinking component.

The Feeler provides the fuel for creation. In the words of Sonia Choquette:

> *Without passion there's no gas in the car. You cannot create on the intellectual level, only on the feeling level. That's the spark that starts the process of change. It's the catalyst, the click over, and if you have no passion there will be no spark. You do not create what you want, you create ultimately what you really desire.*

To live life from a firm foundation, your efforts must come from a place that integrates all aspects of your consciousness. You will come from your center of power if you process your life though your inner Doer, inner Thinker, and inner Feeler. Much like the pyramids that are said to have innate ability to produce power, the Conscious Triangle delivers power to you when you integrate all three aspects at once, find stillness, reason, and power. When you fully understand your feelings, process the situation or endeavor through your intellect, and take appropriate action, you use all of yourself in the process. When you act based on an understanding of your feelings and think before you act, again, you use all of yourself.

When your thinking gives you a clarity about your feelings

that in turn enables both passionate and logical action, the results naturally follow. A person who operates in the integrated center of the Conscious Triangle will more readily tap into his or her own power. The result will be a marked improvement in quality of life as well as success on every level.

Let's consider a few examples.

Example #1 — Starting Your Own Business

Take the person who wants to start his or her own business.

Feelers have an advantage in connecting with what they want to provide for others—they have clarity about what they want to do, what service they want to give.

The challenge for Feelers is that without using the Doer and Thinker, they don't know how to create a viable entity that can provide for them in a financially meaningful way—survival becomes a real challenge. How can Feelers process their strong feelings through the intellect and develop a business (that provides a profit) such that they do what they are passionate about in a way that provides enough for them to continue in that passion? Without developing the Thinker and Doer components, this can create a lifelong challenge.

Feelers don't generally have an understanding of their own self-worth and consequently don't charge enough for their services. They end up in a downward spiral that takes them further away from their passion because they can't provide for themselves. This issue can be decisively addressed either with lightning speed or as slow as flowing molasses, according to our choice.

The advantage of Feelers is that they have more than

enough passion to make their business and life successful. The disadvantage is a lack of understanding of the value of the product or service provided and of the mindset of self-valuation and self-esteem. Typical doubting questions might include:

"How can I go about charging for that?"

"How can I expect to be worth that much?"

"How can I possibly take a day off?"

"Why don't I get people to come to me—do you think anyone would show up?"

Thinkers, as rational, logical people, will continue to ponder a business idea for far too long, with the faulty rationale that if we think for long enough, we can find another business that might be better. This process can go on interminably. Thinkers have a harder time connecting with their passion—it may take years to figure it out.

The Thinker has conceptualized where the money comes from, how the business could work, pitfalls and challenges, opportunities and windfalls. The challenge is finding enough passion to put behind the venture. The Thinker struggles to find enough excitement to get started.

Thinkers need to find a way to connect with their passion, to get in touch with the Feeler such that they discover a business that "feels great," that they are "passionate and excited" about.

The advantage for a Doer is that he or she will engage, get things up and running, and secure an order or a customer long before the Thinker or the Feeler. We can identify Doers because they are a blur of action—they talk fast and think fast with speed and alacrity that most people stand back and applaud.

While busyness and productivity have value, there are unique challenges for Doers. Doers have to ask the tough questions:

"Is all this productivity worth anything?"

"Am I too busy to have a life?"

"Do I have any balance or even understand what that means?"

Balance lags far behind, even in the face of results. It's easy to identify Doers as they never sit still. In starting a business, Doers might not even recognize the potential like Thinkers would nor connect with it like Feelers would. They would simply begin and engage.

Now let's get specific. Nancy, a single mom raising two children, needs to supplement her income. She also must maintain flexibility in her schedule to take care of her responsibilities as the primary caretaker of the kids. Before the children, Nancy obtained her license as a Certified Massage Therapist. Even though her license expired, it would not take much to bring it current again. The problem is that historically, despite a love for the healing arts, Nancy never made enough money doing body work. It never felt right to charge much, certainly not to her friends. It never felt right to make clients come to her, so she spent a lot of time and money driving to and from appointments. It never occurred to her to have a two-tiered price structure, with an extra charge for outcalls. Ten years later, despite her passion, she wonders if she can make it work.

In case you haven't figured it out, Nancy's dominant component is the Feeler. As a multitasking mom, she has a fairly strong Doer side as well. The Thinker lags a bit behind.

With a beginning understanding of the Conscious Triangle, Nancy realizes that she had never made a plan—she just did what felt right. She did not believe she would have a problem taking action, even though she acknowledged that her Feeler was still more dominant than her Doer.

Nancy sat down and with the help of a friend, took the time to calculate how much money she wanted to make, how much she would have to charge, and how many massages she would need to give in order to make that money. She realized that she would have to charge a fair price and not give her services away—even though the fee structure may from time to time feel uncomfortable. Excited, and armed with a plan, Nancy took action and developed a solid client basis with a predictable money stream that supplemented her other sources of income.

Notice that Nancy was no different 10 years ago than she is today. Her Feeler component still dominates, and in fact, is the very strength that makes her so good at empathizing with others and helping them through her work. By choosing to activate her Thinker she gave herself a much greater chance for success, with obvious benefits. Her Thinker will not likely ever become dominant. However, by using the Conscious Triangle and consciously deciding to tap it as a strength, her Thinker became the integral piece that she used to achieve her goal.

This same process applies to all of us.

Example #2 —
Beginning a New Relationship

Consider starting a new relationship, one that seeks to grow based on shared core values—something with long-lasting potential. We know that for the relationship to work at any meaningful level, core values must be closely aligned. The challenge is that in the early stages of courtship, these core values may not be as easy to identify. We must use the power of the Conscious Triangle to dig them out. We'll examine this scenario from the perspective of each of the three components.

The Feeler, as in any situation, has advantages and disadvantages. The Feeler will recognize the passion and the connection with another much earlier than the Doer or Thinker. While this may be fantastic with a person who is primed and ready for a relationship, for someone else it might create a feeling of "being rushed."

A Feeler will be much more connected to his internal side and will experience excitement, happiness, and optimism. Energy levels quickly surge when a Feeler is introduced to someone that he senses shares his core values.

This should not be confused with a sense of lust that often occurs in first meeting someone or certain sexual overtones that arise in the early phases of meeting another. While this may be a magnificent human experience and one to be honored and enjoyed, in addressing the search for a more permanent relationship, deeper questions must be asked and answered from all perspectives of the Conscious Triangle.

Feelers will react toward the strong feelings that they have toward another. The chances of that other person having an identical reaction for any period of time other than an initial exploration are extremely unlikely. Feelers have the advantage of coming from the spot of integrity about their feelings—a component that is fascinating and interesting, attractive even, and one that seldom leads to a truly negative response. The feelings are clear and obvious.

The Feeler risks self-disclosure. This quality is magnetic. Truth and vulnerability emerge and these qualities draw out a response that is almost always positive. Feelers need to be aware of this power.

However, Feelers need to call upon the Thinker and Doer to find a connection that has the opportunity to bring in the relationship they're searching for. The Feeler has to ask questions about core values. This assumes that the Feeler has identified his or her own in advance. The Feeler needs to know if the other person values personal growth, a healthy lifestyle and so on. While remaining connected to the excitement and energy that only a Feeler can sense, the importance of personal responsibility must be explored.

Feelers who are reading this section right now are cringing and frowning with the thought—feeling—of addressing these issues with someone that they are excited about. Unless you want to waste months or even years of your life, these questions must be asked in order to have any kind of successful relationship.

After tapping the Thinker's ability to analyze all possibilities, the Feeler then needs to call on the Doer. The Doer pushes for these questions on core values to come out. Why wait five years? Let's do it now. Let's bring out the issues now.

By integrating the Thinker and Doer into the process, Feelers have a much greater chance of determining early on whether the other person's core values line up with their own.

The Thinker has advantages and disadvantages as well. The Thinker will consider whether another person matches up in terms of core values. The Thinker will generally have identified his or her own. Because of this clarity, a unique phenomenon occurs. The law of attraction determines that once you set an intention or a desire, you attract into your life people and situations that help you manifest that intention. The Thinker, as a rational or logical being, will not make as many mistakes in pursuing poor relationships not based on core values. The

Thinker will more quickly eliminate the car wrecks than the Feeler and Doer.

However, the Thinker's rational side will tend to avoid risk, play it safe, and reject out of hand many relationships that could be exciting and important under the rationale: "This relationship doesn't make sense." Without the cornerstone of core values established, the Thinker will rarely find a person that matches any of his or her rational criteria. Remember that it's much easier to find a way to reject another, to find something wrong with a person, than to accept and embrace him.

The Thinker needs to call upon the Conscious Triangle for help. The Thinker must tap the Feeler and ask the basic questions:

"How do I feel about this person?"

"How is my energy level in this person's presence?"

"Am I excited?"

"Am I feeling different than in usual situations?"

The Thinker must also tap the Doer to take action, ask questions, risk disclosure by putting himself out there, become available—even allowing the rational, logical aspect to go dormant for a while. By tapping the emotional body, the Thinker can also gain energy to activate the Doer—a win-win generated by using the less dominant components. Again, the key is the integration of the three, the strength of the center of the Triangle.

The Doer's greatest advantage is the willingness to take action, to meet people and try to connect. There is much value in taking chances. Through trial and elimination, a solid relationship can be found. This openness to try is by far the Doer's greatest strength. Activity leads in good directions.

The disadvantage is that the Doer has not considered what activities are most important to her nor how she feels about those activities. The Doer must stop and ask:

"What matters to me?"

"How do I feel about it?"

In other words, the Doer needs to stop and slow down. The Doer needs to integrate the Thinker and Feeler sides, to establish the core values clearly. The Doer needs to ask:

"What type of person brings me joy and happiness?"

"How do I experience joy and happiness?"

The value of taking action cannot be overshadowed by a lack of defined core values. Without a clear understanding, the Doer spends much of her life running—but without balance and happiness. By stopping, analyzing, and spending effort to get in touch with the Feeler, the Doer can then charge back out again, even more excited and with greater clarity—an obviously better place to find a good mate.

As is likely becoming self-evident, the Doer's dominant side will drive action and continue to be the strongest of the three. However, by adding the Thinker and Feeler, the same level of activity yields a greater result and is backed by genuine passion.

Notice that sometimes, directly asking may not reveal a core value. We must observe behavior, consistencies, and inconsistencies and what these reveal. Consider the person who claims personal responsibility as a core value yet has been divorced three times, fails to make child support payments, and has terrible credit.

However, many people may not use the words "personal responsibility," yet take each aspect of their lives, work, and family very responsibly. In such cases it is likely that personal responsibility is in fact a core value though perhaps not identified as such.

The person who claims personal growth as a core value but upon questioning hasn't read a book or been to a course or listened to an audio series, might reveal himself quickly. On the flip side, a person who does not consciously hold personal growth as a core value, yet has self-help books on her bedside table and attends seminars to invest in herself, may simply not use the same nomenclature.

Seeing the health habits of people can paint a picture—is there integrity in the way they live? Do they cook their own food? Do they work out? Do they eat healthfully? Do they talk about it or live it? Do they not talk about it at all because it is so natural to them that they don't need to discuss it? It is important to observe and understand that the way we live often tells us considerably more than words.

Now, as we did in the last example, let's get specific. Bob has been on his own for a long time. After a few failed relationships, he took a break from the dating scene and though he still routinely attends social functions, never seems to find anyone to get involved with. There's always something wrong.

Bob's friends push him to meet people, frequently invite him to dinners and parties. He's a brilliant conversationalist and everybody likes Bob. Unfortunately, Bob can't get past his brain.

Tom, on the other hand, is the direct opposite of Bob. Tom loves everybody, is outward and gregarious and the life of most gatherings he attends. Tom has a new relationship every few months. The problem is that these relationships never last more than at most half a year before Tom is on to the next one. Like

Bob, Tom is not happy. He wants something deeper and more meaningful.

Tom and Bob work in the same office. Though not the closest of friends, Bob finds himself listening to Tom's latest traumatic breakup over lunch in the cafeteria. Bob asks Tom how he never knew these disturbing qualities about the person before. Tom indignantly tells him that he never asked—nor would he. Bob declares how absurd that is and Tom retorts by asking Bob when was the last time he had a date. The conversation ends with Tom challenging Bob to join him at a dance club on Friday night. Bob begrudgingly agrees.

Before we go on, notice the absence of integration of the three components. Tom, a die-hard Feeler, seldom taps his thinking side. Bob, a major intellectual, seldom allows his Feeler to come out. Both are stuck, though they each possess all three components, as do we all.

Bob honors his commitment, shows up at the club, and by sheer force is dragged onto the dance floor. Despite his initial disdain, he begins to truly enjoy himself. In fact, he has a blast. In the process, he notices something very different about Josephine, a woman he had known for years and summarily dismissed for some reason or another. On the dance floor, tapped into his Feeler, Bob sees the same person with new eyes. After the best evening he remembered in many years, he decides to take a chance (the Doer) and asks Josephine out.

Notice the power of the Conscious Triangle at work. Once Bob tapped his other two components and managed his Thinker, he obtained a dramatically different result with the same exact person. The possibility had always existed. Here's the most interesting aspect of Bob's story. Bob never intended to tap his Feeler. It just happened when he went dancing, a "feeling" activity. He obtained a powerful result by default because the principle works. Imagine the results he will continue to gain if he consciously applies the Conscious Triangle principles.

The Conscious Triangle is termed "conscious" because it is a tool available to all of us, all the time. We must train ourselves to use it.

Uncharacteristically, Tom spent the entire evening in a deep discussion with Johanna, a woman that he dated two years earlier before their relationship ended in fire, as was Tom's normal pattern. This time though, he and Johanna seemed to connect on a completely different level, talking about what they truly cared about and asking each other question after question. In other words, knowingly or unknowingly, they were sharing core values and discovering which ones they had in common. Tom later told Bob that Johanna was the most fascinating woman he had ever met.

Notice that Tom's passion, his Feeler, still drove him as the dominant component. However, as he brought in the Thinker, he went on an entirely new journey of discovery, found that there was a much greater foundation than he previously recognized—a foundation of shared core values—and, like Bob, saw the same person he had previously dated with entirely new eyes. He then activated his Doer and invited Johanna to join him for dinner—and another dialogue.

The Conscious Triangle functions as an integrated unit, where all sides must come into play for happiness, balance, and wealth to fully manifest:

To understand your feelings and process them through your intellect without activating the Doer is a tremendous waste.

To act without understanding how you think or feel is equally wasteful.

To intellectually understand something without taking action yields no positive results.

To feel something without understanding its rational or logical implications nor acting on those feelings produces little of value.

The power of the Conscious Triangle is that when we operate from a place of clarity in core values and we feel, think, and act from an integrated place, we hit the sweet spot and our results will astound us.

So what can we do to identify our own primary operating model as well as those of the people around us? Pay attention and listen to your own voice and that of those around you.

From a Feeler, you are likely to hear words along these lines:

"I feel what you are saying."

"I'm so excited."

"I'm so happy."

"I'm so glad."

"I'm so mad."

"I'm sad."

"I'm angry."

"That makes me blue."

The feeling will usually be named in the sentence—*excited, happy, glad, mad, sad, angry*. To identify a Feeler, we must listen for those words. You will better communicate with a Feeler if you use "feeling" words.

From a Thinker, you are likely to hear these types of statements:

"Does this make sense?"

"That's logical."

"I think…"

"My opinion on that is…"

Sentences will contain rationalizations and be largely devoid of "feeling" words. The form of expression is detached and intellectual. You will communicate with a Thinker much better using logic and logical statements.

To identify Doers, you must catch up with them as they are always in motion. They are the people with constantly full plates, always on the phone, never stationary. When asked almost any question, Doers will tell you what they are doing, where they have been or are about to go. Doers will best relate to action and action-oriented statements.

To properly use the power of the Conscious Triangle we must first determine our own primary operating model. Then we can tap the other two components and constantly strive to use them all. The payoff of operating in the Conscious Triangle is that you get to create happiness, balance, and wealth in your life in the most powerful way possible—by processing feelings and actions through the intellect, acting with thought and emotion, and feeling passionate about the process. Your results will skyrocket and your happiness quotient will go through the roof. This is what it means to actualize *the Power of You!*

CHAPTER 6

Live a Blended and Connected Lifestyle

Work is about a daily meaning as well as daily bread. For recognition as well as cash; for astonishment rather than torpor; in short, for a sort of life rather than a Monday through Friday sort of dying. . . . We have a right to ask of work that it include meaning, recognition, astonishment, and life.

—*Studs Terkel*

*S*ince the mid-1990s, I have been a member of the Young Presidents Organization (YPO). The requirements for membership are quite stringent. You can join only if you are the president, CEO, or managing director of a company with sales in excess of $10 million annually and have more than 50 employees, both criteria prior to your thirty-ninth birthday. Its membership consists of 9,000 leaders of the most successful companies on earth.

One of the requirements of all members is to participate in a group discussion meeting called a "forum." Forums get together on a monthly basis for a minimum of four hours. In a forum you are given the opportunity and tools to intimately connect with up to 12 other leaders of organizations similar to yours. You hear their struggles, their accomplishments, and their challenges.

During my YPO experience, I acted as a forum moderator. Moderators are trained in specific skills in order to properly lead the group. Because of my nature, I was keenly interested in what the process of acting as moderator would yield. YPO would regularly survey its members to make sure that the organization met everyone's expectations. The need most commonly expressed by the 9,000 members was balance. Consistently, through all my years of membership, it has always ranked as the number-one issue.

My role as the forum moderator gave me interesting insights into human nature and my own understanding of balance. One of the protocols for the forum experience consisted of beginning each meeting with what we called an "update." The updates lasted between 5 and 15 minutes each, depending on the time and attendance at the meeting. It was mandatory to not discuss your vacation, where you were going with your family, or other trivialities.

Forum protocol required that each update consist of the following:

- What is happening in your life?
- What was the most important thing that you would experience in the next 30 days and why was it important to you?
- What feeling could you associate with it?

When this protocol was strictly followed, the updates were magnificent. An intimacy resulted for both the listener and the presenter. This lesson applies particularly well in the analysis of balance.

To the degree that members discussed their feelings and expressed what they felt about the happenings in their life the updates flowed. The ability to self-disclose created true intimacy—the only way to connect with others in a meaningful way. I realized as the forum moderator that what people truly sought was not balance, but connecting. They wanted intimacy. They wanted to be heard.

To the degree that people describe balance as an issue in their life, I would propose a new concept. Balance as historically understood is not what we really want. What we want is a *blended and connected lifestyle*.

Before we define a blended and connected lifestyle, let's revisit several recent premises that have gained widespread popularity and yet, I believe, are inherently flawed.

The Old Balance Model Defined

Balance came to the forefront in the 1960s or 1970s, the first time that the working person attempted to achieve a sense of equilibrium between professional and personal life. The traditional model involved toil for 40, 60, or 80 hours a week at work, then an attempt to make up for that lost time with family in the late evenings or from Friday to Monday.

The historical notion that we can be one person at work and another at home needs to be dispelled once and for all. It is outdated and inapplicable in today's demanding, high-speed world. Still, many hang onto it, mostly to their personal detriment.

How many of us have heard a friend or colleague refer to her "work personality," implying that at home she was someone different? Some even seem proud of the idea and this begs a fundamental question: "Who's the real person?" When confronted, the general reply comes back: "Well, I'm both people, the work person at work and the home person at home."

In digging deeper, most imply that they wear some type of mask at work, one that hides or obscures their genuine self. In theory, this two-person, one-body concept may have made sense in the not-too-distant past, when work was dictated more by geographic location and circumstance than by active choice. However, upon closer examination, whenever any stressful situation arose, only one of the two personalities manifested consistently. The intellectualized two-person concept disappeared and only one real person showed up—implying that the bifurcation never held water in the first place.

For example, the "party animal" outside of work may show up in a button-down shirt at the office during the week. However, if he has few personal boundaries on the weekend, he will in all likelihood suffer from the same condition on the job, even though it may be well hidden.

The Flaws in the Balance Wheel

The classic balance wheel that equally divides life into X amount of time at work, Y amount of time for personal life, and Z amount of time for community or spirituality does not work either. Most people seldom get to the third component and argue that the balance they seek is between work and home.

More often than not, sacrifices are made on the home front, not at work. The balance skews from equal thirds in theory only, to a more realistic fifty-fifty between work and home, to the reality that whatever work requires comes first. Personal life gets mostly the leftovers. In other words, the whole balance wheel division has never been equal, and is largely a mythical creation. Why is this?

Simply stated, the underlying assumption of this type of balance is flawed. It implies that we must constantly make tough choices between personal life and work—a negotiated peace treaty between the home front and the work front. This implication stems from a lack of clarity in our core values and our life's purpose.

Suppose you make a lot of money in a job that no longer challenges or fulfills you. What do you do? How many people have you heard of that are "just getting in their 20 years" or "putting in their time" until retirement? What happens when the pension or retirement fund is lost by the corporate entity that they entrusted? Now what?

Suppose that your work is fulfilling but under its present circumstance provides no practical way to make a reasonable living. Many people have accepted the myth that self-denial, giving to others at our own expense, or continuous self-sacrifice without a reasonable return is an acceptable method of living. This only rings true for those who wish to take an oath of poverty. Sadly, most people have not taken that oath yet exhibit the practice anyway. Again, this points out the absence of clarity in core values.

How many people do volunteer work that they dislike in order to meet some outward appearance? How many parents make sacrifices for their children that they resent yet tout their own praises or seek approval from spouse and friends about those sacrifices? These types of behavior cannot lead to balance.

Quantity Time Does Not Work

Another outmoded idea with respect to balance is the concept that spending "quantity" time with family or loved ones can make up for lost time. Consider the person who ignores family for weeks or months on end with the justification that the time will be made up on the month-long family vacation. He wants to claim that this sudden dose of quantity time will restore balance to the family.

This concept of quantity time is a fallacy. It cannot work because it does not take into consideration the needs of each individual person. A month-long vacation with family may be commendable and even enjoyable. However, it would be more appropriate and sustainable, certainly a greater contributor to the family's pursuit of happiness, balance, and wealth, to connect on an intimate level when each family member most requires it.

Quantity time attempts to put a Band-Aid on the obvious gap in ordinary living—sort of like drinking gallons of water on a given day and then none for three in a row or gorging with food on weekends to then starve throughout the week. The human need for intimacy is ongoing, not something that the lack of which can be restored with short-term oversaturation. Only clarity in core values can drive daily activities that meet this pervasive need.

Quality Time Does Not Work

This leads us to another flawed concept, that of "quality" time. Quality time has been defined as reserved time for child or spouse, on a schedule such as 6:00 to 7:00, when you try to be ready to listen to them. This fails to take into consideration that the other person may have needs and wants at some other time, a time perhaps convenient to her, but inconvenient to you.

Quality time creates the excuse that says you do not have to deliver intimacy or connectivity when others need it. You simply put them in your schedule and everything will work out. In today's demanding and high-stress world, this can't work. We need intimacy when we need it, not when it fits the Day-Planner.

While there is much to be said for scheduling and making a loved one a priority, this cannot act as an excuse for disconnecting the rest of the time. Quality time does not work because it does not take into consideration *when* the needs of another may arise.

The Nature of Work

The nature of work has dramatically changed. The advent of the personal computer has brought both individuals and companies away from the mainframe and tethered style of previous decades. The Internet allows people to stretch even further from the geographic location of their office, plant, or factory. It removes the need for a main office, certainly prevalent until recently.

Many of us work from home, far away from the main corporate location. Most don't labor from 9:00 to 5:00 anymore. Advancements like instant messaging, e-mail, and other technologies make it easy for people to get tasks accomplished whenever convenient for them. The cell phone gives us even more freedom, away from traditional roles.

The low cost and ease of mobility has made it easier for us to travel anywhere and has further contributed to a need for updating the notion of balance for 2006 and beyond.

Balance Needs an Extreme Makeover

The purpose behind balance has been broadly revealed over the last 30 years. People who want more balance in their life are after something specific. Balance, in itself, acts as a red flag, a red herring that requires those affected to ask themselves this fundamental question: "What am I really after?"

My contention is simple: People want their needs heard and acknowledged by others in a meaningful way, especially those that are important to them, and people want to feel connected. None of these needs and wants is a function of time.

Balance does not have to be a zero sum game—if I give here, it takes away from there. What is needed is a new model and a new understanding of balance—balance as a blended and connected lifestyle.

The Blended and Connected Lifestyle

The blended and connected lifestyle means there is no difference between the professional you and the personal you. Only one seamless individual makes up the bundle of joy, enthusiasm, and creative power that has always existed in you. The fact that you sometimes produce better work in one area versus another does not make you a two-headed, one-body monster. *The Power of You!* is more easily discovered when you work from a blended, holistic, and complete self rather than a bifurcated or split personality.

If you live life based on core values, then your daily, weekly, and monthly activities are driven by those core values. It's impossible to have a work or professional personality different from your personal self. It's just you. We don't switch personalities and who we are in different roles or geographic locations.

A blended and connected lifestyle can also be described in contrast to what we historically know. Most of us have grown up with a large gap between our parents at home and our parents at work—seemingly bifurcated personalities. Dad got into a suit and tie, went off to a job somewhere, and did work that most likely had nothing to do with the types of things that he felt passionate about. Mostly, the work was directed by outside circumstances. For example, if you grew up in a rural area, you became a farmer. If your father worked in a factory or in the mines, it was likely that you would follow in his footsteps. If your mother was a homemaker, that's what you were destined to do. The pull was primarily in the direction of repeating parental models. In today's knowledge era, you have many more choices about your career path.

The children of the 1960s and the post-boomer generation have looked at their parents' model of living and for the most part rejected it: "I'm not going to do it that way." However, it's unclear whether the decision of "not doing it like our parents" has resulted in better choices. For the most part, all that has been accomplished is the establishment of a desire not to imitate the old model. We have not necessarily figured out a better model.

We see family members who hate their work go to a dreaded job every day. We see family members drink or medicate because they hate their careers. We see families break up due to dissatisfaction in the work place. All of these circumstances lead to one conclusion: "That can't be me." This statement plants a seed that pushes us in the direction of actually replicating the exact same scenario unless the negative thought is replaced with something else that says: "Here's what I want to be." This declaration must include a clear understanding of one's core values and a decision as to what we choose to do and who we do it with based on those core values.

For example, if we understand that our core values are personal growth and personal responsibility, we must find a career path where we are not one person at work and another outside of work. Rather, we must learn to express those core values in both arenas.

The old model used to be: "I'm on at work. When I'm home, I just want to turn off." This doesn't work anymore. A blended lifestyle requires us to mix our work with our family and our community demands based on our core values—who we are regardless of where we are. The only measuring stick is core values—what we declare as important to us.

If we want to achieve happiness, balance, and wealth, we must be doing something that we feel passionate about, that aligns with our values. Otherwise, we will never find the energy to create the staying power necessary to achieve those high standards. Furthermore, if modern society dictates that work can happen 24 hours a day, why not have it be work that we enjoy? If not, work will suck the life out of us.

The Need to Connect

Whether one of your core values is having intimate adult relationships or not, everyone has a desire to be connected to others. It is the reason we are social animals. It is a reason to a greater or lesser degree that we get married. It is the reason we have families.

Being connected is a primal aspect of the human experience. Everyone needs to be heard and seen for who they really are. With new skill sets such as those set forth in this book, today's connected lifestyle allows us to do this in a short amount of time, in stark contrast with the old model of balance that required us to "spend time with each other in order to be in balance."

"Blended" means that there is no bifurcation between work or professional life and personal life. There is only one life, based on and driven by core values. The connected lifestyle means that you live connected with each and every person important to your life. You acknowledge that there is a human desire to connect, that the desire to create intimacy, to be seen, heard, and acknowledged, is a critical personal need.

To live a connected lifestyle we need to develop the awareness that to connect with another individual does not require a tremendous amount of time. With concepts like quantity time and quality time around for so long, it is easy to fall under the assumption that to connect with people, you must spend hours and hours and hours with an individual. Using the skill sets already detailed in previous chapters, risking self-disclosure through feeling words, quality communication, and so on, one can quickly connect with another individual.

In a successful blended and connected lifestyle, an integrated individual uses the three components of the Conscious Triangle to process these core values fully to ensure that life is lived productively both at work and at home. The two fronts become one.

Flowing from a few e-mails on the computer at first light, to breakfast with the children, to a stop at the office, followed by an adjustment at the chiropractor, to a luncheon with a significant other, a meeting, a track meet, and an evening conference call to finish the day blends work and personal into one. The key is to base daily activities on stated core values.

For example, people who measure their success in terms of how many mouths they feed during the holidays through volunteer work may spend the entire year focused on the target of Thanksgiving and Christmas without any regard for any other tangible reward. They feel excited at all of the aspects that go into those events, planning, preparation, fund-raising, and so forth. All of these activities align with their core values. As a result, they are happy and energized month after month and feel elated when each year they exceed the meals served in the previous year.

The bottom line is: "Are you leading your daily life based on your core values?" In processing life through the Conscious Triangle, personal and professional life are not independent of each other, but rather are blended. The passion for work matches the passion for life; the Feeler, Thinker, and Doer come together on both fronts. If we have identified and are dedicated to our life's purpose, it's fairly easy to blend the two.

Here are some contrasting examples:

Historically, people had to plan to leave the office to even make a bank deposit. In a blended lifestyle, that's simply an errand to be added to the list of "to-dos" as life is being lived.

Historically, people went to the gym before or after work—never at a time that would interrupt office hours. In a blended lifestyle, we take time off in the middle of the day or whenever it makes sense based on work load, family obligations, and so on.

Historically, if you wanted alone time with your spouse, you scheduled a "date night." In a blended lifestyle, you might choose to take an entire afternoon off on any given day.

In other words, the bifurcation of work and personal life largely disappears as core values drive how you choose to live your daily life. It is *not* about how much time you spend together, but *is* about how simple and easy it is to deeply connect if you know how.

Consider the example of speaking with a spouse on the phone. You might schedule a time where you talk each day or you may randomly pick up the phone to say hello. A way of quickly creating intimacy is to begin the conversation by talking about how you are feeling. You use words like, "I'm happy," "I'm sad," "I'm frustrated," or "I'm angry" to instantly acknowledge your feeling state to the other person. The only response necessary from the listener is to acknowledge the feeling: "I understand."

This requires that both individuals identify feelings inside of them as they speak to each other. For some, this will prove challenging at the beginning. With practice, it becomes easy and habitual—a natural way of connecting.

The ability to create intimacy is dependent on being able to self-disclose, acknowledge, and express how we are feeling to another individual. It does not require hours or even more than 10 or 15 minutes. Intimacy can be created in rapid fashion.

While staying connected face to face or over the telephone requires a new skill set, the ability to stay connected with the world and whatever is going on in one's life has never been easier. A blended and connected lifestyle allows us to work from home, from the road, while on vacation—or to be on vacation and do a little bit of work. It allows us to create intimacy at any moment, at any time, without regard to where you are, where your office is, or what else is going on in the world.

The blended and connected lifestyle means that your passion for work and life's purpose blend naturally into your passion for family and home life. Your needs for intimacy, to be heard and acknowledged, are met on a daily basis because you spend your life with people who share your core values. You connect naturally, freely, and continually with those around you using new skill sets more appropriate for today's world.

In the process, you uncover *The Power of You!,* and learn to manifest happiness and wealth—and yes, an entirely new model of balance—the blended and connected lifestyle.

CHAPTER 7

The New Religion of Capitalism

Capitalism and communism stand at opposite poles. Their essential difference is this: The communist, seeing the rich man and his fine home, says: "No man should have so much." The capitalist, seeing the same thing, says: "All men should have as much."

—*Phelps Adams*

*F*or much of this book we have discussed old models and systems that no longer work or require serious updating to make them relevant in today's new world. In this chapter we will discuss a model that needs no adaptation to take its rightful place at the forefront of the knowledge era. It is my position that we are entering a new age of capitalism throughout the world, so critical to our futures that it merits reintroducing—both what it is and what it is not.

This book is not an economic treatise, nor is it intended solely to educate you on the principles of economics. However, when a global wave of this magnitude begins to take shape, it affects all of us and we have the choice of positioning ourselves to take advantage of the surge, or of being unconsciously swept away.

The New Religion of Capitalism

In order to unleash *the Power of You!* to create happiness, balance, and wealth in your own life, a greater understanding of the economic systems is required, both the systems that help make success possible and those that make it more challenging. It is imperative to expose and explain all of them so that in seeking to attain those goals, we set the prevailing winds at our backs as opposed to having them buffet our growth. The most favorable of these systems is capitalism.

Before we explore capitalism, let's set forth certain common definitions of the word *religion*. *Webster's Dictionary* includes the following, in pertinent part:

> ". . . any specific system of belief, worship, conduct, etc., often involving a code of ethics and a philosophy."
>
> ". . . any object of conscientious regard and pursuit."
>
> ". . . any system of beliefs, practices, ethical values, etc., resembling, suggestive of, or likened to such a system."

As you can see, in addition to references to God or a higher power, "religion" includes "any specific system of belief."

Therefore as entire societies and countries embrace capitalism, by definition, this becomes part of their belief system, or religion. If individuals do not believe in the system, they will not adopt it. When it comes to capitalism, we are seeing the exact opposite—a widespread, global embracing of it that is shaping the way we live our lives.

The online encyclopedia defines *capitalism* as "an economic system in which all or most of the means of production are privately owned and operated (usually through employing wage labor, and for profit), and in which the investment of capital and the production, distribution and prices of commodities and services are determined mainly in a free market." *Profit* is defined as "a positive return made on an investment by an individual or by business operations." The Latin meaning of *profit* is "to go forward." A *free market* is defined as "a market where all exchanges are made without coercion, all trades are voluntary."

The web site ImportanceOfPhilosophy.com adds a powerful perspective on capitalism that states:

> *It is important to define capitalism correctly because a proper definition is a pre-requisite to a proper defense.*
>
> *Capitalism is the only moral political system because it is the only system dedicated to the protection of rights, which is a requirement for human survival and flourishing.*

The government exists solely to protect individual rights. This is the proper role of government and capitalism should be defended vigorously on a moral basis and not on an economic or utilitarian basis.

Simply put, capitalism is the invisible hand and rising tide that lifts all boats. It is the system that conspires for your success by allowing any passionate thinker who takes action the opportunity to create happiness or wealth for themselves.

The purpose of this chapter is to connect the dots between the pursuit of happiness, balance, and wealth and the role that capitalism can and will play in your future.

The Need for Profit

In some circles, *profit* is a dirty word. Nothing is farther from the truth. In a capitalist system, profit is the positive outcome sought in any venture.

Profit drives economic, political, and moral change. The incentive to create value that others will exchange for another commodity (such as money) drives human endeavor to create tremendous results of all kinds—better food production methods through advances in farming techniques, better sources of fuel to drive society forward, longer life spans through medical advancements, and so on.

Many people have problems with organizations and companies large or small making a profit. A prevailing belief holds that making a profit must inherently mean that the environment is being damaged, workers exploited, or some other negative connotation. We have been spoon fed since early on that everyone deserves to receive as much as the next person and that we owe it to society to not do so much better than our comrades.

This is pure hogwash. All people deserve the right to compete in a free market environment and to make the choice for themselves whether or not they wish to exert more effort, learn more skills, and work harder than average to attain greater results.

Furthermore, in addition to individual entrepreneurs, all organizations seek some type of return on their efforts, a reason to justify their very existence. In most cases, this return is called profit and every business must produce it or eventually perish.

Charities Must Produce, Too

Notice that even nonprofit or charitable organizations seek a return for what they do. A charity must deliver a product or value, whether that value is reflected in the number of beds offered, vaccinations given, or meals provided. There is a necessary product created and delivered or the charity, too, will cease to be funded—just like the business that perishes without profit.

Since profit has been misunderstood for so long, many people have retreated to nonprofits or charitable organizations to keep their minds pure and untainted from the aspects of capitalism they believe they abhor. Often, people retreat to low-paying or nonpaying positions that severely limit their capacity to enjoy happiness, balance, and wealth because of these misperceptions. Unaware of their own core values, they sacrifice their skills and talents for a price below their actual worth under the guise of performing "public service." They falsely believe that charitable organizations are worthier because of the sacrifice or public good they serve. This simply reflects a gross misunderstanding of the reality that every organization must produce something if it wants to survive—charitable and noncharitable alike.

A small company provides a valuable product or service at a fair price that includes a profit for the owner who took the risk and made the effort. A charity creates a value from its product or service—the value of enjoying art at a museum, the value of a powerful sermon in a church, the value of people housed in a shelter. In other words, there is a product that is measurable that is produced by the entity. Whether this product is money for purchasing something or a charitable donation for the tax write-off or the privilege of viewing art, the similarities abound. Unless an entity produces something that the marketplace values enough to continue to support that entity, either through profit in the case of a company or through donations in the case of a charitable organization, the entity will not survive.

A brief description of other models may further help in understanding capitalism. These include feudal states, socialism, communism, and others. We will consider only the economic ramifications of other models and not the politics, with a special eye toward how these models affect the individual and the individual's personal rights.

I n d i v i d u a l   R i g h t s

Why should I be concerned about my rights? What if a government says I have no personal rights? If I can't own anything because the state owns it all, what do I do? If I can't trade with other men or women because I don't own the rights to my own productivity, why should I bother to work hard?

As human beings, we are born with individual rights—the right to choose, the right to think, the right to create, and the right to do nothing. If these rights are suppressed, we cannot express our full potential. Our pursuit of happiness, balance, and wealth is greatly hampered.

Governments should be formed to protect our individual rights, not take them away—including the right to exchange our skills and efforts for fair trade, the basis of free enterprise. Any government that takes away these rights stands between us and our ability to manifest happiness, balance, and wealth. Any government that protects these rights contributes to that pursuit.

The most powerful form of government is that run by the people based on the vote of the people, called a democracy. Democracies are primarily driven by the economic model of capitalism.

Other Economic Models

Speaking historically, in medieval times the land was owned by the landlord. Feudalism meant that the monarch claimed ownership of the land of all of the citizens. The monarch gave titles to other lords in order to collect rent or other concessions. In other words, the economics were completely controlled by the lord.

In the United States, the Homestead Act granted land to people who lived on it and cultivated it in some way. It transferred title away from the feudalistic model that had the lord (read "government") in complete command of everything.

Unowned land became owned land once a person made the commitment to work that land. Once that happened, title to that land could be transferred to the new owner and could only be transferred away by the new owner—not by the government.

Communism seemed to provide an answer for the perceived widening of the gap between rich and poor. One only has to look to the story of Robin Hood to understand how far back dates the mythology of redistribution of wealth from the rich to the poor. In theory, this myth has its own poetic allure. Yet, given every opportunity to flourish, communism has crashed under the weight of communist states' inability to meet the basic needs of their individual citizens—one of which has been the individuals' desire for their own freedom. The gap between rich and poor has always and will always exist as there will always be those who make the choice to work harder than others—the basis of free enterprise.

From 1900 on, communism was considered the latest and greatest economic and political model. Many countries rushed to adopt it without a full understanding. The case was made that a central planning committee could make better decisions for the entire community in every aspect. In examining the timing, the emergence of communism was largely fueled by world crisis—famines, wars, and other sufferings. The movement took hold largely after the Great Depression.

The complete disempowerment of the individual caused the model to break under its own weight. Even the countries that were the largest protagonists, Russia (formerly in the Soviet Union) and China, have introduced a tremendous number of capitalist programs into their system. Russia has converted into a democracy. In China, though communism is the de facto government institution, capitalism is driving the economy.

In more recent times, socialism emerged as a way to govern certain economies. While the political implications will not be addressed in this book, the main economic aspect is that the primary means of production are owned and operated by the state. The premise behind a socialistic model is that the state can better determine the needs of the individual than the individuals themselves. The trust is placed in the state to do what is right by each citizen as opposed to each individual being trusted. Contrast that with capitalism where the trust rests with the individual, as does the responsibility for caring for oneself.

Pure capitalism can also be contrasted with mixed economies, a combination of complete private ownership that coexists with a blend of private and public ownership. There is no country where pure capitalism exists. Even in a country like the United States where capitalism is most prolifically exhibited, there are many governmental programs and management areas that give rise to aspects of a welfare state—certainly a mixed economic model.

The Marketplace Determines Your Worth

One of the essences of capitalism is the individual's right to apply his labor and receive the compensation that the market deems appropriate. The individual can invest the fruits of his labor however he deems fit, with relatively little dilution or resistance from the state. The more an individual can do this, the more the person can apply his craft and true skill sets, whatever those may be.

This model is defined by individuals who freely act in a self-interested way. It is not an altruistic "serve the public good" model, such as can be argued is the case with socialism or communism or present-day liberalism. The individual's passion to act for him- or herself creates the opportunity for anyone to create the happiness, balance, and wealth that they seek. The fuel required to put forth the necessary effort is much more difficult to come by when all actions are supposedly "for the good of others."

It is my firm belief that society is best served by individuals pursuing their own self-interests. This pursuit has created the greatest inventions, the greatest advances in health care, and the greatest technological advances in human history. For most, when trying to serve only the public good, skills and productivity disappear into the proverbial black hole. The lack of a personal vested interest removes or diminishes the fire needed for greatness. At the same time, each individual's productivity must in turn benefit the public or no viable product is created and the individual has nothing worthy of trading for his or her efforts.

Part of the job of government in protecting free enterprise is the safeguarding of the public good—society's best interests.

However, self-interested individuals who benefit from free enterprise are also the first to step up and pay for services that care for the public good (through taxes and so on), far more quickly in fact than if forced to work for the common good over which they had no say or control.

The emphasis of capitalism is on the role of free markets. Free markets promote cooperation among individuals. The liberty to pursue one's own interests stimulates the creation of better goods and services by definition as each individual strives to achieve and manifest more abundantly.

With the advent of the information and knowledge age, all thinking, research, concepts, and resources are available globally, everywhere, to anyone, at the same time. Individuals have both the ability and the opportunity to pursue whatever they want without limits to their own individual knowledge base. In prior centuries, what people could know was completely limited by what was around them geographically and their financial ability to travel to seek out knowledge or bring knowledge to them. Now, all information is everywhere.

One of the end results of the knowledge and information economy of today is that a person can access the most powerful free market in human history, the global marketplace, through the Internet. A key, determinant question becomes: Do you have the self-interest to pursue and apply the information? If as an individual in pursuit of happiness, balance, or wealth you want to go after your passion, whatever that may be, there has never been a time when the barriers were so low and the resources available so abundant. It is literally a matter of logging onto a computer and seeking those resources out.

The Power of You! has never been greater than in this new era of capitalism where your individual right to pursue your own interests is so accessible and attainable.

The Time Is Now

Going back to an earlier example, it is important to note that when the car was invented it was not an instant commercial success. While Henry Ford took the time to produce a commercially viable automobile, the horse-and-buggy industry pundits flat-out decried its failure. A mere 20 to 30 years later, roads were built everywhere. Gas stations sprang up. An entire new economy began to emerge because of this new invention.

Similarly, the telephone completely changed the way we conducted our affairs and eliminated the need for the historically accepted Morse code. At first, the majority of people who heard of a "telephone" made derogatory statements along the lines of: "That will never work." "I'll never use that." But fifty years later, phones ring in every home. Thirty years after that, everyone carries an individual phone on their person. The world has shrunk dramatically because of technology.

The personal computer was invented in 1980. After a few years it began to be used in accounting and productivity improvement. Though word processing technology already existed in the form of a typewriter, within 20 years, the typewriter is as extinct as the buggy whip. As the computer evolves, it becomes more sophisticated and forever changes again by the invention of the World Wide Web. The commercial application of the Web began in earnest in 1995.

If we could travel back in time and invest in the automobile business in early 1900, or hear about the telephone right after Alexander Graham Bell invented the first model, or buy stock in the first offering of Microsoft, would we have done it? Maybe yes; more likely, no.

We need to ask ourselves: Do we want to participate in a new era early on or wait until we are dragged into it kicking and screaming by the inevitable change that will dominate modern society like the phone, the car, and the computer?

There are two types of people roaming the earth: The first type runs the buggy company, and holds on to his horse and carriage business as it diminishes, despite the obvious decline. The second type manages a telegraph business, has the foresight to appreciate that the telephone is so much better technology that it holds the key to the future, and finds a way to rapidly transition into representing the phone company.

The first type is the person who says she'll never use a computer because a fax machine will suffice. The second goes out and buys the earliest available BlackBerry. Which are you? The implications for creating your happiness, balance, and wealth are profound.

The advent of the World Wide Web and its implications for productivity, cost reduction, access to the free market, access to the consumer, access to low-cost vendors and suppliers, as well as numerous other advances has created a new era of capitalism throughout the world. The existence of this new era can no longer be denied or slowed down.

While personal and human rights in many countries may still have a long way to go, the new era of capitalism is driving a movement. Aspects of free market economies are taking over in predominantly communistic and socialistic societies. No government or society in the last 20 years has been free from the influence of capitalism. The power of individuals to create their own happiness, balance, and wealth is occurring in countries like China, India, Russia, Indonesia, and Eastern European countries that previously forbade individualism in any way.

A person in China can trade his labor for financial rewards that did not exist 20 years ago. Capitalism is so new to China that they barely even have a middle class. Seventy years of feudalism and communism led to no more than subsistence living. The slight introduction of capitalism has resulted in the creation of a middle class in less than one generation and China's present economic growth rate exceeds all other large countries. Until recently, the free market component of capitalism was forbidden by the government.

Now, it can't be stopped. The economic free exchange between the hundreds of millions of individuals in China has created such astounding wealth that it has forced the country to create its own capital markets. Why? To invest this money back in other endeavors, even to produce the infrastructure inside China to support even greater free enterprise—in other words, to further support capitalism. Shanghai will soon rival the global financial megacenters of New York and London.

Prior to 20 years ago, the centralized government forbade all of it. The abundance of labor in China and the demand for that labor outside of China formed a new market because of this new age of capitalism. This entire movement was driven with an absence of governmental planning by individuals who sought to address the needs they perceived, acting in complete self-interest. These needs were addressed by emerging capitalists.

Each of us faces many choices—buggy whips or automobiles, telegraph or telephone, typewriters or PCs. We can wait for someone else (a long-lost uncle) or something else (a new governmental structure) to save us or make our lives better. The sooner we realize that no one is coming, the better chance we have of succeeding. The faster we embrace the fact that a wave of enlightened self-interest is breaking all over the world, the faster we will understand the wealth of choices that stand before us. We can choose to ignore the wave and be carried with the masses, swim into it and take a beating, or turn our board around, regardless of our skill level at this very moment, and let the wave help us along or even propel us forward at lightning speed.

There is a belief system washing over the globe. This wave is the new religion of capitalism.

CHAPTER 8

Create Your Dream Life

Success is not the key to happiness. Happiness is the key to success. If you love what you are doing, you will be successful.

—*Herman Cain*

*I*n this new age of capitalism, in order to have the stamina and energy to go after enlightened self-interests, it becomes paramount to work in areas for which we feel passionate. We have to resurface forgotten dreams, tap into the enthusiasm we once felt for areas we cared deeply about, and bring those to the fore using the Conscious Triangle. It is the beginning of creating a dream life, one that will drive us to making the necessary effort to achieve happiness, balance, and wealth. Without the passion, even with the prevailing winds on our side, life can feel like a painful austerity.

How do we do that? To create a dream life, we must stimulate the process of reacquiring forgotten dreams, and become conscious and aware as discussed in Chapter 2. We must ask the questions that sort out our personal core values, as set forth in Chapter 3. To deliver on the life we always wanted, we need to capitalize on skill sets and strengths that we have available at our fingertips, such as those detailed in Chapter 4. We then must combine those with the core values and process our actions moving forward through the power of the Conscious Triangle, tapping the strengths of our intellect, our feelings, and our ability to take action.

The bottom line is that we have to proactively design our own life. We must do the exercises, and take the time and create a plan. This chapter will give you specific exercises that can help you on the path. Please do them. They have no value simply occupying space on this page. They gain immense value when you make them a part of designing your future.

In planning for a dream life, we have to both clarify and declare our core values *and* remind ourselves of those forgotten dreams—what did we love to do when we were five years old? We need to reconnect to the childlike energy and enthusiasm that exists in all of this.

The questions become:

"What did you want to be when you were five years old?"

"What dreams did you have?"

"What goals were connected to the dreams—if you wanted to be a fireman, did you want to help and protect others?"

"If you wanted to be a policeman, was it because you remembered an experience of an officer helping your family?"

"If you wanted to be president, was it because you felt connected to leading and helping a great number of people?"

"If you wanted to write stories, was it because you wanted to share the feelings that you had as you wrote?"

"Did you have a need to be heard that drove you to work for your high school newspaper as a reporter only to then have that dream fade?"

Many reasons exist as to why and how we disconnect from our childlike enthusiasm, ranging from the aging process, to our hardships, to the dream stealers, and so on. This is not the time to stop, self-edit, shut down, or quit on ourselves. It is also not a time for perfection as there is no need for it. We must allow our dreams to come out and call upon the child that still exists inside everyone of us. Let him or her out to play.

There are certain exercises that I have learned over the years that have greatly helped me. They are not to be read and viewed at arm's length but rather experienced in practice. They will cause you to have feelings and thoughts that you never (consciously) knew existed—but only if you actually do them.

Take the physical action to do the exercises. Write or type your answers. Recognize how you feel while you do them. Notice the level of energy you feel on one subject or another. Some will drain you while others will create tons of energy. The key is to play all out.

First Exercise: Create Your Happiness Board

The purpose of this exercise is to help you dream again. (For the original concept of this exercise, which I have significantly adapted and modified, I'm indebted to the late Dr. David Viscott.)

For this exercise you will need the following materials:

- A two-foot by three-foot tag board or a poster-size material that will stand on its own.
- Note-card-size sticky notes.
- Various marking pens.

This is how this works. Using the sticky notes, write down everything you've ever dreamed or thought of doing and everywhere you've thought or dreamed of going. Jot down anything you ever wanted to accomplish. Put each sticky note in big bold letters. These are declarations of your wants, dreams, desires, and hopes. Don't be afraid to be bold.

Use short headlines of 10 words or less that you'll easily recognize later. Use simple statements, not complex paragraphs. Don't judge or be self-critical. Let the *real you* speak.

Fill in the blanks as you repeatedly ask yourself these questions:

I want to _____.

I dream of_____.

I hope to_____.

With a slight variation on this line of questions author Sonia Choquette asks her clients to fill in the blank after the words

I love_____.

As you finish writing each one, slap it up on the tag board and move to the next one. Do this until the whole board is covered with notes of your hopes, dreams, and wants.

Here are a few examples from my own Happiness Board:

- I want to travel.
- I want to go to Russia, China, Bali, Australia, South America, New Zealand, India, Brazil.
- Learn a second language.
- Become a black-belt in a martial art.

- No bosses.
- Control my own schedule.
- Live healthy.
- Weigh 225.
- Bench press 300.
- Run a 10K in under 40 minutes.
- Love my work.
- Have kids (before I had kids).
- Have intimate adult relationships (after I had kids).
- Financial independence.
- My own company.
- Work in personal growth field.
- Coach others on how to do this.
- Live on the water.
- Have a boat outside my back door.
- Play golf with less than a 10 handicap.

There are about 200 others—a tremendous inventory of all the things I wanted to do, feel, and act upon.

The sticky notes bring a physical presence to your wants, needs, hopes, and dreams of which most people are unconscious.

After you have completed this exercise, ask yourself these questions:

- Was this exercise easy or hard? Why?
- Was it fun and full of energy, or drudgery and draining? Why?

- What item on the board surprises you the most?
- What is it on the board you absolutely must do right now?

Take some time to reflect on what is on the board. If you feel comfortable doing so, share the Happiness Board with your spouse or close friend. Ask them whether the things on the board reflect the person they see in you. Ask them if they see any surprises.

After you've had time to reflect on the notes on the board and taken into consideration your core values, consider these questions:

What do the items on the Happiness Board ask of you?
What needs to be done?

An advance technique utilizing the Happiness Board you may find useful is to rearrange the notes on the board as follows:

- What needs to be done in the next 10 years of my life?
- What needs to be done in the next 5 years?
- What needs to be done over the next 2 years?
- What needs to be done in the next 12 months?
- What needs to be done in the next 6 months?
- What needs to be done in the next 90 days?
- What needs to be done in the next 30 days?
- What needs to be done this week?
- What needs to be done today?

Pay particular attention to the items in the 12 months to 2 years category. I have found in working with all kinds of people that the 12 months to 2 years category holds tremendous potential for creating happiness, balance, and wealth for an individual. In doing the Happiness Board exercise people will write down items that are critical to their happiness but that they never find time for. They are always too busy.

Often, especially if they are in line with core values, these items need to be moved up on the "what needs to be done" list because they are the needs that must be met for happiness to present itself.

Second Exercise: The Memorial

Here is another exercise to help you uncover what is truly important to you and how you want to live your life. This exercise requires you to project well into the future, to envision the day of your own funeral and memorial service. This is not an attempt to be morbid but rather an exercise to allow you to tap into the meaning of your life—both to yourself and others.

For the purposes of this exercise you must imagine that you are lying dead in the casket, or an urn, and can hear everything that is said about you on your last physical day on earth. Make sure you have a pen and paper handy to jot down your answers to the questions below.

Visualize the people coming into the church or temple. Feel the mood in the air. What does it smell like? What does it feel like? What music is playing?

As your family begins to come into the memorial service, what are they wearing? As everyone sits down and the minister or rabbi begins to speak of you, what does the story sound like? Is it a story you are proud of? Does it sound like you?

Now it's time for your spouse to speak, and although it's difficult because of the grief, he or she does an excellent job of re-calling your life and what you meant to him or her. What does he or she say? What did you represent to him or her? What did he or she learn from you as a partner for all these years?

Your children are next. What do they say? What did you as a father or mother mean to them? What did they learn from you about being a man or a woman? What did they learn from you about life? What did they learn from you about being a husband or wife? What did they learn from you about listening to their needs, their feelings, their goals?

Your business partner is next. What does he or she say about what you meant to him or her? What did he or she learn from you?

One of your closest friends is next. What does he or she say? What did your life represent to your close friend?

This exercise can help you clarify what is important to you. What you want to be remembered for is a powerful way of un-derstanding and uncovering your wants and needs. The items you jotted down should be incorporated into your core values and help create the specific actions required to create happi-ness, balance, and wealth.

Author Sonia Choquette talks of doing these types of exercises:

> *I call it feeding your spirit. You have a spirit, fed by certain things unique to you, things that revive your most authentic sense of who you are—a walk in nature, a meditation at church, joining a choir, getting a pedicure, especially if you're a man. Feed the part of you that is intrinsically the giver. I believe that one of our assignments as the six sensory leaders of the world is to show people it's okay to love your-self. We don't have that modeled. We come off a spiritual*

system, a thousand years of self-sacrifice as the model for love and caring and sometimes that's an important part, but as an exclusive way of life to the detriment of yourself is no longer going to support the planet.

Once we reconnect with the child within and begin to map out our goals and dreams, the next step is to carefully take an inventory of ourselves. What do we truly love to do now and, with respect to that, what skill sets do we have that can help us do that? Equally important—what skill sets are we missing? Where can we go find them? Whom do we know who might help?

In reaching out for help, we must remember that most people we know see us in the way that they have always seen us. The feedback we get might not serve us. Consider the family system once again. A family member may not have the ability to see that we are seeking a new outcome and therefore need a different kind of advice.

The same logic applies to anyone from whom we seek counsel. We need to carefully filter the source and the message when it comes to someone who knows us and only has the historical filter of who we used to be—not who we are seeking to become. The best intentions make no difference in this arena. Any counsel we seek must meet our objective—a new outcome for ourselves.

Let me share with you an example from my own life that might be illustrative on how you can put all this together.

Scott's Story

I realized years ago that one of my familiars was a sense that I was wrong for wanting a deeper and more intimate relationship with my father, a connection that I wanted since I was a little boy. Unfortunately, he was too busy with work and providing for four kids.

At five years old, I drew the conclusion that I was wrong for wanting that intimacy from him. Sadly, I also came to the conclusion that not only was my desire for an intimate connection wrong, but that I was wrong at my core. It's really the only conclusion a child can draw. Our parents are Godlike, heroic figures to us all. I could never blame my hero. He could not be wrong.

My familiar was that feeling that my hopes, dreams, and passionate desires were wrong and I was wrong for feeling worthy of their pursuit. This kept me safe. It was what I knew. I would not have known how to deal with anything else.

Because of the conclusions I drew regarding my familiars I learned to suppress many other feelings, wants, and desires. As a young boy I coped with this loss of intimacy by substituting it with my desire to be a "good boy." I remember my dad leaving on long business trips every week and asking me to be the "Man of the house"—a responsibility that I took very seriously. As the oldest, I knew that if I couldn't connect with Dad the way I wanted I would make sure that I did what he wanted.

Fast-forward 30 years or so. After consistent attempts to connect with my father on a more meaningful level do not work out, it begins to dawn on me that something else may be in play here. Still, I decide to try one more time.

I was going through a challenging time personally and professionally. As I look back 10 years I realize now how unbalanced and disconnected my life was to anything for which I held a real passion. At the same time, I had begun to do some good inner renewal work, based on a strong core value of personal growth.

I discovered how sad I had been over not having a more intimate relationship with my father and that I was not wrong for
wanting more than I got. More importantly, my wants and desires were not only natural but healthy and I was worthy of having every one of them met.

This change came because I was willing to mourn the loss
of the relationship I didn't have. I had to grieve the loss of my
unmet needs. This was hard for me but definitely worth it. I
could not have done it alone. I needed someone to bear witness
to my suffering. I'm convinced that most everyone needs help
during life's rougher patches.

As I faced this challenging time, trying to make a decision as
to what direction to take professionally, I went to my father who
has been a strong business advisor for me. He counseled me to
get back into the glass business, and make some money—to stop
messing around with entrepreneurial ventures. I believe that he
gave his advice with my best interest in mind, wanting only for
me to prosper. I went to him because I trust his business advice
and counsel.

As result of understanding my familiars, I realized that I
would ask my father for advice and speak to him on business
matters partly to make up for the connection that was missing
with him in other areas. Though his business advice was always
sound, it was never a substitute for the real connection I wanted
and needed as a child. It omitted any acknowledgment of the
power of feelings, passion, excitement, or desire.

In making my decision on a direction in business, I knew
that I had to connect my skills with my passion. My father was
not capable of the type of connection I desired. I was still responsible for my pursuit of my own hopes and dreams. Once I
realized that and grieved the loss of the relationship that I
yearned for but could never have, it was easy to move ahead and

do what I truly wanted to do. First, I had to let go of my familiar of "being the good son," or "doing what Dad wanted for me."

I in no way blame my father for the good advice he gave me. I simply recognize that I was stuck in an old familiar. Once I understood the familiar and grieved the loss of a missed relationship, it was completely cathartic for me to move beyond it. I felt unburdened and could immediately move forward powerfully. The critical epiphany was my understanding of the familiar—regardless of what my Dad did or did not do. Once that happened, the energy and excitement came through me to do what I needed to do. The call became an easy one. "I'm not wrong. My desire to have deep meaningful, relationships is not wrong—all I need to do is acknowledge the strong pull of the familiar, recognize that as an adult I'm not governed by it, and *move on*."

I remembered calling Joe Green, one of the people who wanted to hire me, and telling him: "Joe, my attempt to get back in the glass business was all about me trying to connect with my dad." It felt fantastic to make such an acknowledgment. I'll never forget it, as I drove down the 91 Freeway in Southern California. Though I didn't sense that Joe had any clue of what I was really saying, it didn't matter. It was a statement and a declaration about me and my familiar. I had broken free from it and it felt great to utilize my skills from the present to heal such an old wound.

Take a Chance on You!

Once we uncover our dreams and begin to make them clear for ourselves, we must then risk self-disclosure about our objectives, knowing that we may face a barrage of chuckles. We must look past those to ask others for help. Others can be those we work with, people we may have respected, good role models, and so on.

Almost always, there are two or three people in our circle of influence who have the ability to give us feedback on our real self. Often, we don't know who they are and because of that we need to ask many people for help along the way. We don't know who the "go-to" person is.

The key in wanting to go after a dream or facing an obstacle is to get out of our own way, risk self-disclosure and seek advice. The process and exercise of asking in and of itself has its own rewards. We rapidly learn who can help, who can't, and who will be a detriment.

Some in your circle will give you feedback because they know you well enough to touch on your skill sets and your interests and give you clues as to where the treasure within lies. Remember that the clues to the treasure always seem perfectly clear after the treasure is uncovered. However, during the process, they are far less clear.

You will be amazed at who helps you and what insight they provide. You will also be amazed at those who are unable to help and who want you to stay in your current position. It's your responsibility to discern whom you choose to listen to. You have to take the chance, manage the disappointment, and even take responsibility for allowing any naysayer to condemn your idea or attempt to quash it.

When asked the question, how important are these people in helping you along the journey, Sonia Choquette answered as follows:

Critical. I wrote a book about it called The Diary of a Psychic. *It's all about my mentors; my mother, my teacher Charlie*

Goodman, my teacher Dr. Tolley, and how much influence they played in my life. They helped set my values, helped me find my courage and held me to a high standard. If you have those qualities you should offer them to mentor others. And if you need them, acknowledge you need them and seek the best. Ask. I love to read and develop concepts and understand, but I think there's something critically important to doing it with a live human being. I really think you can't do it on your own.

Scott's Story Continued

About the same time as I had my epiphany on the 91 Freeway in Southern California I had been slowly coming to the realization that I needed do something in the personal growth field. Though I had felt this many times before, this was the first time I could listen to the feeling. The difference was that I no longer felt obligated to be the good little boy and deny myself my feelings. As a result of understanding my familiar, I knew that I could pursue my life based on my core values and I began to make my life's decisions using the power of my own Conscious Triangle.

I started a series of discussions with my good friend, Steve Amos. Steve was also going though a time of personal growth and we shared with each other our hopes and dreams for the future. We had similar backgrounds in business. We both ran large manufacturing concerns in Southern California. We expressed disinterest in returning to our old business roots though we had been financially successful.

We had met in YPO and for many years had a close, intimate adult relationship. He knew of my interest in personal growth from my work as the moderator of our forum group. I shared with him that as the president of my companies I was responsible for results over a wide variety of areas—much like he had been. I drew more satisfaction and personal enjoyment from producing results through people dedicated to personal growth. I loved learning new ways to do things and sharing them with others. Steve shared this love of learning and thirst for personal growth. That common love became the embryo that formed the nascent beginning of ConsciousOne.

Steve's wife, encouraged him to pursue his interest in personal growth. She had been working and writing in the personal growth field for a number of years and had experienced a sense of happiness that she was eager for her husband to share.

After many discussions we came to a point where I remember saying to Steve: "Wouldn't it be great if we could make personal growth our life's work?"

Simultaneously, I began to work on what this business could look like. I considered doing an events business that was geared to the likeminded world of spiritual seekers. I then watched a friend lose over $1,000,000 trying to do something similar and realized that I needed to take the time to truly plan this out, using the tools at my disposal. I methodically took the space and did the work.

By way of analogy of how this can also work for you, I'll share my process.

I began by clearly defining and declaring my core values. I specifically made the effort to write them down—which I highly recommend that you do as well.

Here are the core values I have been living by:

- *Personal growth.* I'm continually and consistently in the process of learning about myself. I read good books, and host and participate in conference calls. I have a coach that helps give meaning and accountability to my efforts. My professional life is all about personal growth and now I write books to share my experiences with others.

- *Preeminence of the adult relationship.* My wife and I share this value. Once we had kids nine years ago, this became an important goal for us both.

- *Dedication to life's purpose.* I'm completely and purposely dedicated to personal growth, my own and that of others to the extent that I can help.

- *Accountability.* In my blended lifestyle I am accountable for my actions and my results. No one else is responsible for what I do.

- *Quality communication.* Because of my work in the personal growth field, communicating my intentions and expectations as well as listening to others is a core value I exhibit daily.

- *Self-disclosure.* I reveal myself and share with others who I really am—in my writing, speaking, and coaching.

- *Reason or Rationality.* Things must make sense for me. Irrational thought or feelings not processed through the intellect are not much beyond the infant crying for Mother's milk, perfect for the infant, very tedious for adults.

These have been my unconscious core values all my life. By consciously choosing them, writing them down, and declaring them, a whole new world opened up to me. By living my life based on these core values my ability to make decisions about what I would or wouldn't do became much easier.

My wife Karen and I started a process of asking ourselves if we were living the life that we wanted. Using our new understanding we began to question if where we lived was the right place. Surprisingly, after 12 years in Hermosa Beach, California, we said no.

We made a list of things we wanted for ourselves in our dream life. It looked exactly like this:

- Large yard, so our kids could play.
- Water out the back door with a boat.
- Open space so we could see the stars, not city lights.
- Safe place for our children to grow up.
- Great schools, preferably public.
- No winters as we both hate cold.
- More affordable as Southern California was expensive.
- Golf club where we could easily play.
- No personal income tax.
- An employment climate hospitable to employers.
- Blue water that takes your breath away.
- Internet business with a home or small office.
- Virtual employees.
- Karen to return to work on her own schedule.
- Financial independence.

The more precisely we defined our daily lives, it became increasingly clear that we were not going to find it in our present situation.

Steve and I had a similar conversation about what we both wanted out of the next years of our lives. He shared with me that he had long ago wanted to move out of the big city life and return to a slower-paced environment. We began to search the country far and wide, through the Internet, through our friends, and by reading articles for the place where we could move ourselves, our families, and our fledgling company, ConsciousOne. At that point, we had no idea where we were going. We did not even have a formal company but the seeds had been planted. The concept of creating our dream life began to germinate.

I know I could not have created my dream life without choosing my core values, employing the power of the Conscious Triangle, understanding my familiars, and using the other tools outlined in previous chapters.

If you are a young person reading this, or someone contemplating a career change, I have a suggestion—find a credible aptitude test and take it. Use it as a tool to help flush out your latent interest. If you can, do so with a professional who can help you interpret your results—an industrial psychologist or other expert who can analyze your strengths and make you aware of them:

What do I really want to do?

What excites me?

What have I dreamed about doing?

What do I want to be doing each day?

What type of work blends my personal core values?

What type of activities do I want to be doing each day?

What activities give me energy, bring me heightened awareness?

If I had $10 million in the bank, what would I be doing with myself each day?

Equally important as what do I want to do is what do I *not* want to do or avoid:

What sucks the energy out of me the moment I even think about it?

What activity makes me cringe at the very mention of it?

What job would I hate doing?

What functions do I despise?

What would I never do in a million years?

What work drains me when I think, read, or talk about it?

What activities take my awareness and glaze it over?

Whatever that is, run from it. Don't do a trial six months. Don't give it a shot. Run. The power of what we *don't* want to do is equally important in clearing out clutter.

By the way, remember from our work on life cycles that the things you love to do or avoid change periodically—every 5 or 10 years or more. For example, during one period you might enjoy traveling 20 days a month, in a different city every day. Ten years later, that might seem like a fate worse than death.

It's important to be open to the reality that we change over time and to not deny that what used to seem exciting may no longer hold appeal. We all have cycles and rhythms in our lives that we must pay attention to.

Ninety percent of seekers begin with the question: "What is my passion?" That's why these tools are so critical to use. Until we get clarity on this fundamental question, the rest is a futile exercise. You get to take the energy of all the ideas that reside in your brain and release it.

This is not to say that we don't also want to pay attention to long-term goals but rather that anyone can get started in creating a dream life right away—and getting started is most often the biggest obstacle.

Now that you've done the work on uncovering the dream, it's the perfect time to bring in the power of the Conscious Triangle. What is your strongest modality? Are you a Feeler, Thinker, or Doer? Which of the three needs to be brought into the equation to create a rounded plan with the maximum chance for success?

It doesn't matter where your strength manifests the most; the process still applies:

First we uncover what we *feel* strongly about.

Next we have to *think* out a solid plan.

Finally we must *do* the necessary actions to carry out the plan.

Let us return to the examples we have touched on in previous chapters.

Assume that we seek to make a career change. After years of working for others with varied levels of success, what used to seem fulfilling has lost its luster. The passion is gone. You decide that you want to strike out on your own. Through the above exercises, you rediscover a passion for personal growth and inner development. You know that you can no longer stay in your corporate position. It no longer sustains or fulfills you and in fact is not part of your core values. Happiness will elude you.

With the power of the Conscious Triangle, you reflect on ideas that you feel passionate and excited about. You bring in the Thinker to process the idea and determine whether it is a job, product, or service that others may want and find value in. Does it make sense? Is there a market? Will the community exchange goods for it? Could you be successful with it?

If you can answer affirmatively, now you bring in the Doer. You create an action plan and begin to execute, all the while keeping the passion of the Feeler to drive your excitement and the logic and rationale of the Thinker to make sure that the action steps make sense.

All of the elements of the Conscious Triangle work together, based on your core values, for you to create your dream life—the ultimate reflection of *the Power of You!*

I'll close this chapter with a final exercise from Sonia Choquette that you can use as you build your dream life. Sonia says:

> *I tell my students to begin to say this particular phrase. The subconscious mind doesn't discern. Whatever you feed it, it will produce. Practice saying this for ten days: "I live a charmed life, no apologies."*
>
> *Be a model of the new way. You do live a charmed life and no apologies needed. It's not socially very popular to be happy. It takes a lot of courage. But those who live a charmed life attract it.*
>
> *The second part is really important, too: no apologies. You might get someone who says: "I'm great," but you don't believe it. But contrast that with the person who looks into your eyes*

and says: *"Thanks for asking, the truth is, I am living a charmed life, it's working out for me."*

Fake it till you make it. In ten days you will be living a charmed life, even if you don't feel that experience in the moment.

Why don't you try this exercise for the next 10 days? It's simple, easy, and you deserve to create a dream life.

In the next chapter we will explore certain obstacles and roadblocks you may encounter and how to overcome them.

CHAPTER 9

Anticipating Obstacles and Roadblocks

Obstacles are like wild animals. They are cowards but they will bluff you if they can. If they see you are afraid of them, they are liable to spring upon you; but if you look them squarely in the eye, they will slink out of sight.

—*Orison Swett Marden*

*I*n the process of creating a dream life, you will inevitably experience rough patches and difficult times that challenge you in many ways, some of them quite unexpected. As we challenge ourselves to grow, occasional setbacks will naturally block our progress. One key to overcoming these challenges is to anticipate the possibility and prepare for it beforehand. This chapter will focus on providing tools to both see potential problems before they happen and overcome them.

Fear

Fear is a perfectly understandable obstacle or roadblock, quite common for most of us. It is primordial and inherent in our species' survival—the classic "fight-or-flight" instinct. Especially in the face of change, fear rears its head because change by definition is unknown. Everyone understands the feeling of fear, though not everyone embraces that you can feel fear and still face it—whatever it is. The feeling can be acknowledged and weathered while one soldiers on.

Sonia Choquette describes it as follows:

I have come to observe that the common denominator that gets in people's way is fear. But we don't talk about fear. It's not culturally or socially acceptable to admit you have it. We go to a lot of trouble to hide it.

My experience tells me that it is not the fear that stops you, it's the hiding of it because that takes a lot of energy. Go at it directly and acknowledge that you are afraid.

People never say: "I'm not afraid." They'll immediately admit it if asked and given permission.

Once you acknowledge the fear, all that energy that you use to hide it is freed up.

She offers us a great exercise that I have personally used and highly recommend. Ask yourself this question: "If I were not afraid, I would _____" and fill in the blank.

Sonia further explains:

The exercise "if I were not afraid, I would . . ." gives you permission to go straight to the heart of what's important to you. It's like trying to hold an elephant behind a door and all of a sudden just opening the door. Go in and look in the room, see what's in front of you. You can't look at your heart if you're busy holding fear at bay.

Too often I've seen the fear of the unknown challenge cause a person to capitulate or quit. It can cause some to not even start. We can use fear to hide from choosing our core values—a way to continue our life in hiding. We can avoid being accountable by living in fear and pointing fingers. At the end of the day, fear must be confronted. While it might not always disappear, by basing our decisions on our core values and using the skill sets we have learned, we can make our way through it.

S u c c e s s   a n d   S e l f - S a b o t a g e

Success creates its own obstacles and opportunity for sabotage. Consciously every person asked whether they want success will always answer affirmatively. However, if present or historical circumstances have displayed a lack of success, lack of wealth, or lack of balance, then that becomes familiar—what you are used to.

As you discover *the Power of You!*, you will begin to create an environment for sustained personal growth and you will experience positive change that is unfamiliar to you.

Do not underestimate your ability to return to circumstances of lack or struggle. With new skills you will achieve greater results. While you consciously attempt to convince yourself that you always wanted success, the first time you attain it will cause anxiety, discomfort, and confusion. It will seem very unfamiliar. Do not underestimate your ability to sabotage this unfamiliar state and return to the state that is familiar.

Here is an example: A salesperson is accustomed to $2,500 per month in commissions from his or her efforts. After acquiring new skills, the salesperson begins to receive commissions of $10,000 per month. While conventional thinking would be that this is fantastic (and it is), few of us recognize what is going on inside the person historically used to making only $2,500 per month.

In addition to the elation, many other emotions come into play. The majority of people fail to sustain a new level of success or commissions and will return to their previous income or perhaps a little more—a more familiar place.

Unless you understand the power of working from your core values, processing through the Conscious Triangle, and that you must actively design your dream life, the desire to return to the familiar will guarantee self-sabotage. You must know in advance that sometimes the journey will become uncomfortable and you will have to persist despite the unfamiliar change.

The key to growing and sustaining change is acknowledging the feelings that occur inside of you. For most of us, the struggle to get to the next level is familiar while maintaining the change is not familiar. The tendency becomes to sabotage the change to return to the struggle. In order to maintain the change, we must understand the feelings that made the struggle necessary in the first place. We address the familiar, tap into our core values, acknowledge the old, and move on—even in the face of those who want to hold us back.

As Sonia Choquette points out, your change affects everyone and this can cause resistance:

> *You will run across people who will resist your change, the Debbie Downers, the people who say: "Oh, God, you're going to do that—it never works out, I can't believe you're doing it."*
>
> *When they show up, you're on your way, that's a good indication, a test. Every time you want to evolve you're going to invite test. Recognize it as a test and be happy to take your test.*
>
> *People you haven't talked to in a long while will show up. All that is representative of the old starts coming out of the woodwork. It shows and confirms that you are in the*

process of changing. You should embrace it and say: "great, it's working."

Don't be wounded and sensitive if people aren't on your side because they don't want you to change. That would mean that they would have to look at themselves.

Personal Beliefs on Success

Prior to understanding core values, your personal beliefs that were imprinted on you as a young person and that you have assumed over the years can be a tremendous obstacle to your success. What if during your past, through learning or experience, you began to believe the following:

"It's okay to be successful, as long as it is not too successful."

"It's okay to be successful, but not more successful than my parents."

"It's okay to be successful, but not more successful than anyone else I know—other family members, my church, my community."

"People don't applaud my success; they scheme for my demise."

"I shouldn't climb too far up the ladder or get too big for my britches."

In addition to these limiting beliefs, you may have adopted a number of others:

"Life is a struggle."

"Life is supposed to be hard."

"If life isn't difficult, there must be something wrong."

"When things are going well, watch out, because something bad is coming around the corner."

"Life is never supposed to be easy and enjoyable."

If you grew up with anyone in your family, parents, grandparents, or others who were influenced by the Great Depression, these limiting beliefs might hold large sway over you:

"There is not enough for everyone."

"There might not be enough for me to get any."

"I don't deserve to have my share."

"There never will be enough."

"There may be enough for others, but there will not be enough for me."

If you grew up in a particularly controlling environment, you might have adopted a belief that limits your ability to move forward and take action:

"The product or idea is not perfect and therefore we can't put it out there."

"If it's not right, I had better not put my name on it."

"I'm not ready yet (nor will I ever be)."

"I need to study this more."

"I don't know if this will work."

Notice that all of these beliefs are limiting, self-defeating beliefs that contribute nothing but anxiety, fear, shame, guilt, and other negative feelings that reduce any opportunity to gain happiness, balance, or wealth.

Scarcity mentality creates a self-fulfilling prophecy. If you hold the belief, "Nothing ever works for me," you will take the actions to make that so. This belief is defeatist at its very core.

Suppose you hold the belief (the reverse zero-sum mentality), "Everyone else gets what they deserve but I don't." This assumption creates a burden so heavy that you resign yourself to carrying it forever—and it becomes true. You manifest what you tell yourself.

Suppose instead that you choose an exciting, high energy, creative way of living your life, one that is the entire opposite of the self-defeating belief system described above. Your beliefs might instead state:

"I am deserving of success—happiness, balance, and wealth—and my success is determined by how far I wish to go."

"There are no limits to my success that can be placed by anyone other than myself."

"Life is to be enjoyed and filled with happiness."

"When conflicts arise, I know I can handle them and gain something from the experience."

"There is more than enough of everything for me and everyone else—and it's my responsibility to claim it."

"I don't need to be perfect—I want to share with the world what I have now."

"I will grow and offer more as I do and get better each step of the way."

There is no benefit to adopting or continuing to accept self-defeating beliefs. If you have the choice of programming yourself with thoughts of abundance or beliefs of scarcity, why would you ever choose to wallow in self-defeating beliefs? Your subconscious can't tell the difference. Only you are responsible for what you are feeding it.

Return to your Happiness Board. Remind yourself of your dream life. Then tell yourself that you deserve it.

Passion versus Position

One insidious obstacle that you may encounter is a low degree of energy for any new endeavor you choose—career change, new business, or whatever. It's important to employ the power of the Conscious Triangle to find out how you feel about the venture. You need high energy and must be able to bring that to your new undertaking. If you don't feel that energy, it should be a huge red siren and an indicator that perhaps you are doing this for other reasons, a sense of obligation, out of an old familiar rearing its head. If the endeavor feels confusing or unclear, treat this roadblock as an important warning signal.

Dr. Nathaniel Branden talked in an interview about the need to be very conscious of our choices, to make sure that we fully understand what we undertake:

> *The more aspects of any situation you see clearly, the more possible options you have for what to do. Living consciously or mindfully, is the key element of successful living.*
>
> *We interact with our environment. We interact with people. We interact with projects and challenges. The more*

clearly we see, the more effective our behavior will be. We need to see and to make seeing our highest priority. That's what it means to live consciously.

To create sustainable change, you must have a level of passion and excitement that can carry you through conflicts and speed bumps that will inevitably come up. You should stay away from ventures that drain your energy before you take on the task. If a contemplated endeavor does not create a feeling of high energy, reevaluate. See if you might not find something else more appropriate. Check in with your core values.

Here is an example: A woman who works for a big-three accounting firm for many years consistently saves her money and gets herself into a safe and comfortable financial position. Periodically, she dabbles in her true passions, real estate investment and writing. She experiences her job as unchallenging and unsatisfying. She secretly dreams of quitting her job and beginning to write and invest in real estate more actively. The passion and excitement comes out in her voice when it comes to investing and writing. She asks the question: "Should I quit my job?"

It is crucial to realize where your passion is, where your true interests lie. This person needs to find a way to move in that direction. This does not mean quitting the job tomorrow or other rash behavior but rather recognizing the source of the passion, the high energy that comes along with that, and finding a way to move toward converting those dreams into reality.

Sonia Choquette described in an interview the need for passionate commitment as follows:

I had a client that is an extremely talented man about 32, a gifted writer, who was completely shut down and stuck. I gave him a whole list of actions he could do to initiate his life. Then he challenged me: 'That's all well and good but, what if I'm not committed to this, how do I know I'm going to get results if I really get emotionally committed to this? How do I know that it's going to work out?"

I answered: "By the same reason that you're so emotionally committed to doing nothing because that is working out perfectly. You've got nothing. That's where your commitment is."

He started laughing and admitted that it was true, he was committed to doing nothing. Look at your results. You get what you give.

The accountant in the earlier example faces the same challenge. To do nothing will yield no results. It's imperative that she tap into her passion.

Present Circumstances

Many people blame their current circumstances for their inability to manifest a different type of life. They tell themselves the following: "If it weren't for my (insert present circumstances here) I would be pursuing my passion, going after my dreams, etc."

Present circumstances could be anything:

Mary believes that she has intuitive gifts and would like to work in the healing arts. However, she claims that her husband doesn't believe in it and she does nothing.

Leo declares that he's ready to pursue his passion to start his own business but can't because of the hurricanes, a divorce, and a sick child.

Kimberley, a married mother of two, wants to go after her interest in real estate. The excitement shines through in her voice when she talks about the idea. However, she states that she has no money to invest in the required courses.

Sonia Choquette makes the following observation:

People think and get stuck because they believe that thinking about something is the equivalent of doing something. So they don't do anything. If you want to change your life and your vibrations, you have to do something different. You need to introduce action or you will see no change.

No matter what your present circumstances are, no matter how real or challenging, they need to be addressed. Everyone has them. At the end of the day, these roadblocks can either stop you from your pursuits or be directly challenged in going after your pursuits. No one is immune.

Once you discover passion based on core values, present circumstances present less of a roadblock as the heightened desire to pursue your passion takes over. This passion can render present circumstances from roadblocks into mere speed bumps.

Scott and Steve's Story

Sometimes we face roadblocks almost impossible to overcome, yet somehow people still do. Sometimes the roadblocks are built of our own actions or inactions, other times as a result of the actions or inactions of others. I would like to share with you a couple of experiences that first appeared as devastating roadblocks I could never have anticipated.

As ConsciousOne really began to blossom toward the end of 2003, my partner Steve and I initiated our search for the ideal place where we could operate our business. We had consciously and purposely created an Internet-based business so that we could move it to our dream location once successful.

Becoming profitable took quite some time, as with most businesses, and we proceeded for a long while without compensation of any kind and without any assurance other than in our guts that the business would ultimately succeed.

Because of the risk and because of Steve's significant financial investment, we were elated when we finally started to draw some income from the business and begin our search for the perfect place to live and work.

We searched the Internet. We talked to friends. I put out an e-mail request to the Young Presidents Organization for information. As described earlier, we created a detailed checklist of things we wanted to experience and enjoy as a result of this anticipated move.

We searched throughout the entire country and then began visiting places. For reasons that are now obvious we began to focus on the northwestern panhandle of Florida. Though very different than Southern California, we felt that it was ideal for our new blended and connected lifestyles.

After multiple visits alone and with our wives, we fell in love with the town of Destin, Florida. Following much due diligence, we agreed that we would move the company and our lives to Destin. With the help of the Internet and additional travel we both were soon making offers on real estate.

On Steve's second or third visit with his wife Terri he experienced some discomfort with his leg and foot. In fact, it was so painful that he needed medical attention both in Destin and subsequently upon his return to Southern California. His doctors initially thought it was gout and were going to treat it with the appropriate antibiotics but decided to run just a few more tests.

The tests revealed that Steve had a very aggressive form of prostate cancer. His prostate specific antigen (psa) test score was frighteningly high. A subsequent biopsy revealed that he would need both surgery and radiation treatment if he wanted to live more than five years.

When the initial feeling of shock and disbelief finally wore off, the devastating diagnosis terrified Steve, his family, all his friends, and me. Steve and I had helped a close friend through a similar diagnosis less than a year ago. It seemed impossible that this could be happening again.

After this potentially devastating roadblock reared its ugly head, Steve sought more information from his doctors about the surgery and subsequent radiation treatment. He looked at the timeframe of both therapies and we talked about our future. We decided to move ahead with our plans for ConsciousOne. We shared an intensely firm belief Steve's health issue was difficult but temporary and that he would come through his surgery and radiation treatment. We agreed that our business and move was of critical short-term and long-term significance to us both. Our core value of commitment to personal growth was manifested perfectly in ConsciousOne. It was not easy. More than a few tears were shed. Often, worry seemed more prevalent than hope.

Many people would have put off the move. Others may have

stopped moving forward with the business. We relied on our feelings, intellect, and actions based in solid core values. We made clear and conscious decisions.

As the realization of the diagnosis took effect I recall that we went though myriad emotions. We felt scared, sad, worried, energized, hopeful, and determined all at the same time. The most difficult and sad moment for me was hearing how scared Steve was about his mortality and leaving his kids without a father. He knew his son A.J. would miss him terribly. He was very emotional about leaving his two daughters without a father. We had many discussions leading up to the surgery. None could be more heartfelt and profound than listening to your best friend contemplate the end of his life and how it would affect those left behind.

The period prior to the surgery was most challenging for both of us. We did not know how the prostate surgery would affect Steve's quality of life. We were not sure if or when he would be back at work. We ended up treating it like a vacation. Not that this was anything fun or enjoyable, but we had in fact planned our business so that either of us could be away from it periodically. We resolved to treat Steve's absence as a vacation. I would cover his duties during the recovery time. We consciously chose to handle this roadblock as a temporary obstacle and gave it no more weight than it deserved or could take from us. All the while, we honored our feelings, and did not turn them off or run from them.

The subsequent radiation treatment ended up being worse than the surgery itself. The radiation treatment essentially burns up the insides of your body and drains you of any strength. It took three months, a veritable marathon compared to the sprint of the surgery. It was the most difficult time for Steve and for me.

Because the radiation treatments were so draining he could work only half days—an amazing feat in itself. He shared with me on many occasions that even a few hours of work gave him a break from thinking about the cancer, his health, or the next radiation treatment. I welcomed whatever he could give. It felt good to take on the extra burden and help my partner through a difficult time.

If we had been working in some other business, one not based on our core values, I'm not sure if the venture would have survived the stress of a potentially terminal illness. Oddly, as I look back, it seems that in a very powerful way the business in fact sustained us—a pure, clean, energy-giving force that balanced the awful cancer and its aftereffects.

Maintaining the extra load was not a burden for me. It was my badge of honor. For Steve, I think that growing a business based in his passion also sustained him in his darkest hours.

I'm thrilled to report that Steve's psa test shows no sign of prostate cancer. Losing Steve would have been devastating to me. We have developed a relationship that is so rare among adult males, based in respect, intimacy, creativity, and productivity. I love him. While he is not 100 percent back to his old self yet, his 95 percent is better than most people's 100 percent.

No one could have anticipated the roadblock we experienced with Steve's health. Nevertheless, we did not let it deny us our dreams. It would have been easy and even understandable to postpone our move or quit the pursuit of ConsciousOne because of Steve's cancer. We chose not to. That choice has made all the difference.

Not all obstacles are life threatening or as dramatic as cancer. Often times they are small, insignificant multiple little speed bumps that cause you to veer off your chosen path. With tools like core values, the conscious triangle, and living consciously you can find your way back on track, able to overcome the obstacles and roadblocks that in the past precluded your creation of happiness, balance, and wealth. That is what it means to reveal *the Power of You!*

CHAPTER 10

Time for Action

The best years of your life are the ones in which you decide your problems are your own. You do not blame them on your mother, the ecology, or the president. You realize that you control your own destiny.

—*Albert Ellis*

$\mathcal{A}$t the end of the day, in order to get a result of any kind, we must take action. If we want a different result than we've had until now, we need to take different action. The tools in this book can help you on the journey, can provide clarity, means, methods, and much encouragement. But none of that means anything without action.

Dr. Nathaniel Branden put it best in an interview:

Many people don't take responsibility for their own goals, the accomplishment of their own aspirations or the solution to their own life problems. They dream of a rescuer who somehow will spare them the necessity of thought or struggle, who will somehow make things right, somehow redeem the pain of childhood, somehow make one feel better about oneself or about life. I tell my clients:

"No one is coming."

"No one is coming to rescue you."

"No one is coming to lift from your shoulders the benefit

or the burden of responsibility. We are all beings who need to take responsibility for our lives and wellbeing."

"No one is coming to save us."

It's a tragic, stupid life to sit around blaming other people and waiting for somebody to say: "Oh poor, poor, poor chap here. Let me make everything right."

It just doesn't happen. I've been practicing therapy a long time. Naturally along the way, one looks for clues, for key turning moments. For me, the day that I would always name first is the day that a person finally gets it—that no one is coming. That if he or she doesn't change in some way nothing is going to get better.

This chapter is a call to action. It's about taking the tools in this book and applying them to your own life. I can't give you the magic formula that will cause you to choose your core values and declare them—both to your self and others. I can't pinpoint your familiars, nor tell you which is your dominant modality within your Conscious Triangle. What I do know is that creating your dream life is both a journey and a process. It involves wonder and work. My hope is that you will make your own adventure less about intellectual understanding and more about the resulting experiences and feelings you uncover as you go down the path.

Nathaniel strongly reiterated this point:

A lot of people come into the world or reach a certain point with skills that once upon a time were exactly what the situation required. Horror after horror, they're finding out that what they knew these years past isn't needed now. What's needed now, they don't have yet. That again is the challenge of continual growth, both mentally and intellectually.

We must both begin the journey and commit to it for the long term. Nothing comes easily, especially when it comes to an endeavor as large as making dreams come true. If anything, this modern age demands more than ever before from each of us. Today, to flourish, we must seek.

One final quote from Nathaniel on the new age we live in:

It demands learning, continuous learning, a lifetime project. We need growing competence at interpersonal social skills, emotional intelligence, social intelligence, the ability to work effectively with other human beings and good communication skills, written or oral. People who have high levels of verbal and oral skills, rise much faster in an organization than those who do not. All sorts of intellectual tools are in demand and needed now, if you want to make it in any big way, in an information age economy.

He implores us to develop ourselves and I couldn't agree more. The opportunity is in front of us. We just have to show up.

The ConsciousOne Story

At the time we were creating ConsciousOne the Internet was rising from the ashes. The dot-com bubble had burst. Capitalism and free markets worked as they should and businesses without real products or services would not survive. The fundamentals of doing business on the Internet would prevail and soar like the phoenix.

Steve and I decided we had to build something on the Internet. We felt that it was the future of business and we had to take action to capture it, to ride this new wave. We wanted the content and the people we worked with to be both enjoyable and of the highest caliber.

We routinely turned down authors because of absurd demands and poor attitudes. ConsciousOne birthed from the idea of living our lives with passion, not heartaches or aggravation.

In retrospect, we knew that if we could find a venture in which to pour our passion, we would succeed. For the first time, the Artist within needed to step forward and take charge. The Thinker and Doer had to take a back seat.

My strength in figuring out how a business can work made putting together a plan almost second nature. That both Steve and I truly knew how to do.

Tapping into feelings proved much more challenging. This is a much more recent and budding skill. Only in the past five years have I consciously worked on developing the Feeler side of my Conscious Triangle. It has made a world of difference. In fact, this recent pursuit came about only when I realized that my Thinker and Doer never took into consideration the underlying feelings—and this would never lead to a fully actualized life.

In studying our core values Steve and I identified that personal growth held one of the highest spots for both of us. We asked ourselves how fabulous it would be if we could make personal growth our life's work. We continued to dream, to investigate, and put that intention into the world. Then we took action.

We researched the field on the Internet. We found out who the players were. We pulled out our old personal development books and manuals from courses we have taken and discussed what we liked best about each one. We identified which types of work fit us best and which ones felt less like a match.

We took further action and enrolled in a business speakers' event that was to be held two weeks later. When we went to the event we asked everyone possible what they were looking for. Because we coincidentally knew the event organizer we learned as much as we could about the financial aspects of the event and the business.

Without this massive and immediate action, we never would have learned a number of necessary lessons. The event organizer shared how much money he lost—in excess of a million dollars. We could not have asked all the participants what they truly wanted. We would have made countless mistakes and put ourselves on a much longer learning curve. The difference was in the massive action. This event steered us away from large speaking seminars and toward the Internet, where we could both control costs and go after our passion.

Steve, my partner, is a tireless networking machine. He never hesitates to pick up the phone and call someone to ask a question or return a call to anyone seeking his help. Just as we concluded that the wrong action would be to jump into the personal growth speakers' business, we got a referral from a friend of Steve's who said he had a new Internet idea and wondered if we'd take a look at it.

There was no business plan at that point as we were still in the research phase. Upon further exploration we learned that the idea consisted of creating an online course for *Conversations with God* by author Neale Donald Walsh. We were thrilled to have the opportunity to work with Neale.

Our excitement led us to take further action and contact other authors in the personal growth world. We shared with them our vision and what we were trying to accomplish. Our business skills served us well in these discussions, fueled both by our passion and our ability to move quickly and decisively. We soon garnered more authors and the support of prominent publishers in the personal growth industry. It seemed that everyone loved our concept and immediately understood what we were doing. Many had a strong desire to help.

One of the biggest obstacles a business can face is where to find its first customers. We knew that as an Internet venture we would live or die by our ability to grow our database to a significant size. At that time we had a database of 7,000 individuals. We knew that for our efforts to make any kind of meaningful difference, we had to get it up to 50,000 interested members.

Again, we took action on multiple fronts. We asked each of our authors if they would mail some of our other programs to their list. The agreement was that everyone one would reciprocate with each other, with ConsciousOne coordinating the efforts. Each author had the right to approve the content of the program and the message prior to any mailer being sent.

We created a free product called a WisdomFlash. Each WisdomFlash was based on a particular author's course and presented in flash media for viewing, hearing, and experiencing over the Internet. The intention of WisdomFlash was to create a moment of peace and relaxation for the viewer—an *aahhhhh* moment. The WisdomFlash gave those of us who live in the Internet world a temporary pass from e-mails, spreadsheets, and pop-up ads. If successful, the viewer would feel an instant emotional bond with the content and our company.

Notice the common theme that keeps repeating itself: action, action, and more action. Sonia Choquette said the following:

Without action you're not honoring your thoughts or your feelings. Everything is in vibration. The world is built on vibrational patterns, on the mental plain, the emotional plain and the physical plain. And there is change in three levels.

The first is the mental plain which is like the car.

The second level is the feeling plain, the equivalent of the gas.

The third plain is action and that's the destination. You can have a car idling away and going nowhere without action.

You're stuck idling away. You have to do something.

My experience has been that if you're in doubt, just do something—any action, paint something, sing something, dance something, put on a new colored tie as a symbol that we're changing—anything, because the subconscious mind thinks in symbols and not words. If you put on a new tie, that's my symbol that something's new, and the subconscious says, well, now we'll start creating something new.

The effect of taking action with our WisdomFlash messages had profound ramifications. When we sent our first Wisdom-Flash messages out we included a special button that allowed the viewer to share it with a friend. Our members did just that. New people joined ConsciousOne in droves. Our database started to grow and grow.

We paid enormous attention to customer feedback. Our members loved our online courses and enjoyed the online journals and exercises they contained. Then they made requests. They sent us e-mails asking if there was a way to hear from and possibly speak to the authors who created the work they studied. We created conference calls that now form part of most programs offered on ConsciousOne. Providing our members with the opportunity to interact with the authors has significantly increased the quality of our available content.

We constantly asked for help. We contacted other companies and told them what we were doing and asked them if they would share our content with their audience in return for us doing the same with ours. This simple action has grown our business more than any other—a classic win-win reciprocal relationship.

We never got stuck in perfectionism before putting our materials out there. We did not wait until every single item in an author's program was perfect before we launched it. We knew that there would always be one more thing to fix or improve and we used the feedback from our members to make those improvements. We put ourselves and our content into the world. Then we continually revised and fixed each program based on feedback from the users themselves—a model that we still follow today. Our members are vocal and willing to share what they like and dislike. We always listen. This feedback loop has given us an opportunity to create 10 times better products because we listen to our members rather than think that we know more than we do or delay launches in search of false perfection.

Our passion is our business. Every day I work with people who model the behaviors and core values I embrace. ConsciousOne continues to grow at an astounding 50 percent per year. Our database exceeds half a million members dedicated to personal growth and spirituality, with over three million more people in our affiliate circles.

Not a single day feels like work. Living my core values, working through my Conscious Triangle, enjoying a blended and connected lifestyle has contributed to a happiness, balance, and wealth that in the past, I only dreamed about. Equipped with new tools for a new era, I took action and made the dream come true.

I urge you to take the time to honor the potential within you, to do the work necessary to define your core values, learn the needed skill sets to flourish in the information age, and take advantage of this incredible period that we live in. The prevailing winds blow strongly at your back and will carry you to far-distant shores, the shores that only your dreams can create.

I invite you to join me on this journey, a journey of self-actualization, of manifesting all that you can be, playing full out and enjoying the ride. Make your mark in this world. Leave your imprint. In all your endeavors, on your terms and by your definition, I wish you the greatest happiness, balance, and wealth. It is all there in front of you, ripe for the taking, ready and available.

All you have to do is bring out *the Power of You!*

ABOUT CONSCIOUSONE
(WWW.CONSCIOUSONE.COM)

*C*onsciousOne provides online courses and programs in the areas related to personal growth and enlightened spirituality. Our programs generally consist of an online course with text, audio files, video clips, personal journals, collateral materials such as books, CDs, and DVDs, conference calls with the author, and many other special bonuses.

The online courses generally include written text on a subject along with specially recorded audio and video inserts. As a course participant, you have the chance to read the messages, see the authors speaking on your screen, and hear them through recorded audio messages that reinforce or add to the course. Most courses also include interactive exercises to help you absorb the material.

The conference calls provide the opportunity for you to actually speak with the author. This special feature sets ConsciousOne apart from other personal growth companies and consistently ranks as the best part of the membership experience. The calls last for approximately an hour and are always recorded so that you can listen to the call at your leisure if you can't make the appointed time.

Most of the courses also have chat or message boards so that you can interact with other program participants to further enhance your experience. Nothing makes your take-home value greater than sharing your experience with likeminded individuals.

A few of the authors presently available on ConsciousOne are: Dr. Wayne Dyer, Sylvia Browne, Dr. Sonia Choquette, Arthur Joseph, Dr. Doreen Virtue, Morrie and Arleah Shechtman, Dr. Nathaniel Branden, Neale Donald Walsh, Terri Amos, Marc Allen, Chris Howard, John Holland, Shakti Gawain, Drs. Gay and Kathlyn Hendricks, Dr. Ava Cadell, Barbara Marx Hubbard, James Ray, and Kathy Smith. New authors and content are added nearly every month.

Scott Martineau, president and co-founder of ConsciousOne, has been consulting with organizations to improve individual performance throughout his professional life. His new book, *The Power of You!*, is offered as a course at www .consciousone.com. He is also available on a limited basis for keynote speeches and private coaching.

Visit the consciousone.com home page to check out the wide variety of currently available content. Once you arrive on the home page, find the ConsciousOne media player and open it up by clicking on it. From this media player you can listen to samples of authors' content, conference calls, and much more.

ConsciousOne has also created a new media experience called WisdomFlash, defined as a "modern day poem in the heart" delivered over the Internet. There are presently over 30 WisdomFlashes for your enjoyment just for enrolling at www.WisdomFlash.com.

From less than 7,000 members and two courses in 2002, consciousone.com has grown to over 500,000 members and more than 20 programs, with more added each month.

Brief descriptions of the current course offerings follow.

ConsciousOne
225 Main Street Suite 2
Destin, FL, 32541

CONSCIOUSONE
COURSE DESCRIPTIONS

Courses are listed by author and are available at www
.consciousone.com.

Wayne Dyer
Power of Intention

*Change the way you look at things and the things you look at
will change.* When Wayne Dyer read those words many years
ago, he had no idea how long a journey it would be until the
release of his book, *The Power of Intention*. His extensive research has revealed intention as the force in the universe that
allows creation to take place. His book teaches you how to access the field of energy called intention to begin co-creating
your life.

Ten Secrets for Success and Inner Peace Course

Finally, ten secrets to success and inner peace put into a course!
In this course, Wayne Dyer's secrets are elaborated upon and
put together in a way that, if mastered and practiced on a daily
basis, will guide you to a sense of tranquility. This is an extremely valuable course for anyone who has decided to consciously be on their life path. The course is enriched with
exquisite lessons, audio clips of Wayne, a personal journal, and
WisdomFlash!

Ten Secrets Daily Planner

This is a powerful daily planner based on the Ten Secrets of Success and Inner Peace by Wayne Dyer. Plan each day around these 10 principles and see your life transformed each and every day.

Sonia Choquette
Psychic U: Level 1—Activating Your Sixth Sense and Living an Extraordinary Life Course

This course was inspired from Sonia Choquette's book, *The Psychic Pathway*, and her 25 years of teaching people around the world to use their sixth sense. In this course, Sonia shares her profound insight about what it really means to be psychic. She explains through her lifelong experience that we are all psychic and that it is our God-given natural ability to utilize our sixth sense.

Your Heart's Desire

What is your hearts desire? Whether you are seeking true love, financial stability, a new job, or health, you are about to acquire a simple secret to creating life as your heart desires it to be. No matter what your heart's desire is, large or small, you can make it happen by following the recipe to your dreams that Sonia will reveal.

Nathaniel Branden
Six Pillars of Self-Esteem

In this course, Nathaniel Branden presents the culminating achievement of a lifetime of clinical practice and research. In this penetrating course he conclusively demonstrates the importance of self-esteem as it relates to our health, personal achievements, and positive relationships. The Six Pillars of Self-Esteem, action-based practices for daily living, are explored and simple but powerful exercises are provided to strengthen your self-esteem. If you are a parent, the sections on children and self-esteem in schools is a must.

Chris Howard
Turning Passions Into Profits Special Package

Plug in the winning mental mindset, eliminate financial fear and anxiety, and tap into your endless flow of spiritual abundance in just 27 minutes. Finally, there's a guaranteed way to overcome your financial difficulties and achieve the goals you want. It's based on a combination of established time-tested results and the latest technology of study of the mind.

Arthur Joseph
Vocal Power

Want to change the way people respond to you? This is the key to what's been holding you back your entire life! Amazing secret weapon hoarded by movie and TV stars, singers, business leaders, and politicians—skyrockets your self-esteem, transforms your voice in minutes a day, eliminates fear of public speaking and commands instant respect from the people you meet.

ConsciousOne Course Descriptions

James Arthur Ray
Science of Success

As soon as you begin working with the Science of Success, you'll discover how to balance your life and create your own prosperity, because as soon as you get started, you'll discover one of the most important laws. Your past does not equal your future! James Ray is a leading expert on the psychology and science of success. He has devoted his life to helping ordinary people lead extraordinary lives. And now it's you turn to experience this quantum leap forward.

Doreen Virtue
Healing with Angels

Includes four recorded conference calls with Doreen, immediate access to Doreen's online course Healing with Angels, the complete Connecting with Angels Kit, the complete Archangel Oracle Card Deck and Guide Book, a copy of Doreen's book *Healing with Angels*, hand-selected angel articles, and the special free bonus book *Divine Prescriptions*.

Sylvia Browne
Mother God

People like Montel and Larry King often ask, "Sylvia, what do you really want out of life?" And she always answers the same way. Her life's dream is that you be open to the spiritual world around us. That you become in touch with your guides and that you learn to trust them to lead you to the magical life that awaits

194

your call. Each day, people like you attain their fondest dreams, true love, health, and abundance. Help her dream come true as you open up the door to your new life.

Journey of the Soul: God, Creation and Tools for Life Course

Does God exist? Was the world created or did it evolve? Where am I in the big picture of the universe? Most people have asked these questions, but have no clear answers. God, Creation and Tools for Life is the first of the Journey of the Soul 3 course series. In this course, Sylvia Browne shares her 40 years of study on these issues, drawing from multiple research sessions with her spirit guide, Francine. We are assured that God will respond to all questions—our job is to ask the right ones and be receptive to the answers we receive.

Ava Cadell
Twelve Steps to Everlasting Love

Dr. Ava Cadell is known around the world for giving people a more complete perspective on relationships, intimacy, and sexuality. Her ability to talk to different groups is demonstrated by her appearances on programs as diverse as *The Tammy Faye Show* and *The Howard Stern Show.* "Love is the best prescription for good health," says Dr. Ava. She is a board certified sexologist who has taught widely to groups of all ages. Reporters have dubbed her the "Goddess of Aural Sexes" (that's not *oral*), because Ava teaches that sex is between the ears, not just between the legs. "If everybody listened to Dr. Ava's relationship advice, this world would be a much better place and we would all be having great sex!" says Ms. Terry Murphy, Emmy Award–winning journalist and host of television's *Hard Copy*. Dr. Ava believes passion is at least 50 percent of a relationship. ConsciousOne is delighted to make Dr. Ava's program, "Twelve Steps to Everlasting Love," available to you.

Shakti Gawain
Creative Visualization

This course, based on the best-selling book that has sold over 6 million copies worldwide, is filled with audio, visual, and printed text meditations, affirmations, and techniques that can help you use the power of your imagination to create what you want in your life. In the course you will be taught how to change negative habit patterns, improve your self-esteem, reach career goals, increase prosperity, improve your health, and much more.

Ridgely Goldsborough
The YoungSlim Lifestyle

Rediscover the secrets of youthful vitality and long-term health, say goodbye to those extra pounds now, and finally feel healthy! What if you could wake up in the morning, look in the mirror, and discover that the bags under your eyes, the extra fold under your chin, and the drooping posture had been replaced by a vibrant and dynamic bundle of energy, smiling back at you full of life, and suddenly you realized that this beaming, radiant person was you?

Gay & Katie Hendricks
Attracting Genuine Love

Attracting Genuine Love gives you a new way to consciously create the kind of love you want. Through a special process that awakens a flow of unconditional love inside yourself, you open a space for an unconditional lover to come into your life. Attracting Genuine Love teaches a unique set of experiential processes to give you clarity about what you most want in your partner. By the end of the seminar you are empowered to manifest a close relationship by conscious attraction rather than stressful pursuit.

Conscious Loving for Couples Course

Conscious Loving for Couples and Singles teaches you how to perform a very practical kind of magic. The skills you learn in this course will put your relationship on the right track, keep the love flowing day-by-day, and keeping you out of those inevitable tough places we occasionally find ourselves stuck in.

Conscious Parenting Course

The Conscious Parenting Solution is a self-paced Internet course that teaches you how to use four simple, powerful techniques. The Four Foundation-Tools bring harmony and simplicity to the most complicated and stressful job you have in your life. With the right tools, even the hardest job gets a lot easier.

John Holland
Psychic Navigator Package

Includes three live conference calls with John, his *Psychic Navigator* book and Audio Meditation CD, the new Psychic

Navigator online course, and John's newest CD, filled with audio meditations that will allow you to jumpstart your psychic medium abilities right now.

Barbara Marx Hubbard
Emergence

This course discusses a new spiritual path, a path for all who wish to make the transition to the next stage of evolution, the transition to becoming a Universal Human. In this course you will find a wonderful guide to experiencing your higher self. In simple terms this course examines, "How do I get from where I am to where I want to be?" In clear and concise terms it lays out a roadmap to a better here and now as well as a better tomorrow.

Neale Donald Walsh
Communion with God

Most people believe in God, they just don't believe in a God who believes in them. Welcome to a course that will make you a believer. In order to do so, you must look beyond the Ten Illusions of Humans. When you recognize these illusions, you can change the way you think. This course discusses the experience of Oneness with the Divine and describes a path to that experience, a pathway through our Ten Illusions, to ultimate reality.

Conversations with God Book 1

Make your entire life a conversation with God! This is the first experiential online course specifically designed to embody the

CwG philosophy. Change in our world starts one person at a time. We believe that the deep changes you can experience from this course will allow you to be the change you wish to see in the world.

Finding Right Livelihood and Re-creating Yourself

This course is based on one of the most astonishing books of our time, *Conversations with God*. All of the concepts found in the *Conversations with God* books revolve around a central theme, "The purpose of life is to re-create yourself anew." This course takes that theme and renders it functional. You are about to be given the key to the universe. You will then be handed the tools with which to fashion the life for which you have always yearned: the life of your dreams.

On Abundance

In the Conversations with God Abundance Course, you will gain a deep understanding of how the benevolent universe works to provide us with the abundance that is naturally already ours. Through the study of each lesson, meditative practice, journal entries, prayer, and a weekly action, you will uncover *who you are* and the power to create anything you desire in your reality.

The New Revelations

The New Revelations tells us that all behaviors are the result of beliefs, and we cannot make lasting changes in behavior without addressing the beliefs that underlie those behaviors. The TNR course provides numerous exercises, discussion, and spiritual journaling opportunities to examine and determine the relevance and value of the beliefs that have been underlying your experiences, possibly since childhood.

The Mastery of Learning

The Mastery of Learning imparts an understanding of how your body works and why you are not as effective at learning as you can be. With your new understanding, far more effective learning techniques become available to you that flow naturally as your mind/brain/body are wired to function, thus giving you immense increases in learning ability.

Marc Allen

Let a lazy, Penniless California Dreamer show you how he built a multimillion-dollar publishing empire! You see, Marc understands people are naturally skeptical and he doesn't want people to think this is a course where you just form a positive mental attitude and the world beats a path to your door. Marc believes you're going to need to take simple action steps. If you do that, nothing more, nothing less, the results will astound you.

Terri Amos

Do you find yourself angry and frustrated with life? Do you want to run away? Do you feel buried in responsibilities and overwhelmed with day-to-day situations? If you do, you've lost your connection to God. Terri would like to share some tools with you to help you re-create that connection in her unique Cleanin' Out the Crap package deal. It will transform your life!

Christen Brown
Star Power

Have you ever wanted to express yourself with remarkable confidence? Or speak to a roomful of people and have them lock on to your every word? Do you want the kind of charisma where people look at you and whisper, "Who's that?" In this compelling program, internationally renowned communications coach, Christen Brown, shares her secrets for building unstoppable self-confidence and mastering your expressive power.

ABOUT SCOTT MARTINEAU

*E*arly in life, **Scott Martineau** turned his entrepreneurial passion into a desire to help people. After graduating from the University of Minnesota with a degree in Political Science he stormed into the business world ready to make his mark. His early career was in sales. Marketing and management positions quickly followed.

His interest and pursuit of knowledge and new ways to live life to the fullest was evident early in his career as he took courses and programs whenever he could. His leadership positions in the glass and packaging industries provided great financial success yet left him wanting something more.

Scott took his expertise and experience and co-founded an Internet-based company called ConsciousOne. He realized that his greatest passion remained in the development of people and he formed a company whose mission would be to create courses in personal and human development.

In less than four years ConsciousOne grew into the largest Internet-based personal growth course provider in the world, with such visionary authors and leaders as Neale Donald Walsh, Dr. Wayne Dyer, Dr. Nathaniel Branden, Sonia Choquette, and so many others.

Today, Scott continues to pioneer the field of human development as a luminary and leader whose innovative thinking helps millions around the globe break free from outdated shackles to fulfill their true individual potential.

He lives in Destin, Florida, with his wife, two daughters, and their dog, Prince.

INDEX

Abandonment:
  as childhood familiar, 22–28
  failure to challenge as, 38
  lack of accountability as, 73
Abundance mentality, 11–12
Accountability, as core value,
    41–42. *See also* Expectations,
  holding high
Action, importance of taking,
    179–188
Adult relationships, as core value, 39
Amos, Steve, 151–152, 155,
    173–176. *See also*
  ConsciousOne
Awareness, *see* Consciousness;
  Conscious Triangle

Balance in life, *see* Blended and
  connected lifestyle
Blended and connected lifestyle,
  105–119
  core values and, 113–119
  flawed premises about, 108–113
  people's wish for, 106–108
Branden, Nathaniel:
  on accountability, 42
  on conscious choices, 169–170
  on expectations, 70–71, 73–74
  on feeling, 86–87
  on goals, 40–41
  on information age, 4–5
  on self-disclosure, 57
  on taking action, 85–86,
    180–182

on thinking, 87–88
on willingness to challenge,
  37–38

Capitalism, 121–135
  benefits and spread of, 122–124,
    132–135
  contrasted to other economic
    models, 128–129
  individual rights and, 127
  profit and, 123–127
  self-interest and, 130–131
Challenge (willingness to), as core
    value, 37–39
Charitable organizations, profit and,
    125–127
Childhood feelings, *see* Familiars
China, 129, 133–134
Choquette, Sonia:
  on dream life, 145–146, 150–151,
    158–159
  on fear, 163
  on feeling, 90
  on learning curve, 54–55
  on passion, 170–171
  on resistance to change, 165–166
  on taking action, 172, 185–186
Circumstances, seen as obstacle to
    creating dream life, 171–172
Citizenship, as core value, 35
Communication, as core value,
    42–43
Communism, 128–129
Compassion, as core value, 33–34

Inner renewal, as core value, 41
Internet, pace of change and, 3–4, 8–9

Joseph, Arthur:
  on benefits of challenging, 38–39
  on life cycles, 53
  on quality communication, 43
  on vocal awareness, 21–22

Life cycles:
  dream life and, 156
  planning for, 51–55
Life's purpose, *see* Goals
Lifestyle, *see* Blended and connected lifestyle; Dream life
Limiting beliefs, 166–169
Love in the Present Tense (Shechtman and Shechtman), 22–25

Memorial, creation of, 144–146

New age, *see* Consciousness; Information age
Nonprofit organizations, product and, 125–127

Obstacles, to creating dream life, 161–177
  beliefs about success, 166–169
  example of, 172–177
  fear, 162–164
  passion versus position, 169–171
  present circumstances, 171–172
  self-sabotage, 164–166

Passion, dream life and, 169–171
Personal growth, as core value, 36–37
Personal health, as core value, 36

Personalities:
  in blended and connected lifestyle, 113–115
  different at work and home, 108–109
Personal life, *see* Blended and connected lifestyle
Personal responsibility, 74–77, 180–182
Profit, 123–127

Quality communication, as core value, 42–43
Quality time, 111–112
Quantity time, 110–111

Reason/rationality, as core value, 33
Relationships:
  adult, as core value, 39
  Conscious Triangle and start of new, 94–101
  second-order change and, 20
  self-disclosure and, 59–64
Respect, as core value, 32–33
Responsibility, taking personal, 74–77, 180–182

Scarcity mentality, 9–12, 168
Second-order change, 17–20
Self-awareness, *see* Consciousness
Self-disclosure:
  as core value, 34–35
  family system and, 68–70
  risk of, 55–64
Self-examination, 20–22. *See also* Core values
Self-sabotage, as obstacle to creating dream life, 164–166
Shechtman, Arleah:
  on core values, 31
  on familiars, 22–25, 65–66, 67
  on second-order change, 19–20

Exclusive
Behind the Scenes Interviews
of *The Power of YOU!*

Bonus Audio Package
Absolutely **FREE** with Every Order

Enjoy over 10 hours of Special Audio Content
Included at No Extra Cost with Your Order

(Content valued at over $279 if sold separately!)
Behind The Scenes Bonus Page
www.consciousone.com/bonuspage/bonus.cfm

The "behind the scenes" interviews were conducted by author Scott Martineau with the intention of giving his readers additional insight and clarity regarding the content of the book. In the interviews you will hear some of today's leading thinkers in the field of personal development comment and expand on the concepts presented. These interviews were conducted with the sole purpose of giving the purchasers of *The Power of YOU!* a bonus—exclusive material not found or sold anywhere else. It's our special way of saying thank you!

This material is available exclusively to purchasers of *The Power of YOU!* and is available nowhere else. The recorded bonus material contained within the member's area of this web site will continue to expand on your understanding of *The Power of YOU!*—providing you with the perfect complement to your reading. Best of all, the "behind the scenes" interviews will be continuously updated—adding to your ability to take action and create happiness, balance, and wealth.

These once-in-a-lifetime recordings allow you to experience the "behind the scenes" interviews directly on your PC or laptop. Replay them whenever you need an extra "boost" of inspiration or need your spirits lifted. The running time of each interview is almost *1 hour in length*—making this special audio library easily worth several hundred dollars if sold separately!*

The interviews include enlightening and motivational recorded conversations between the author of **The Power of YOU!** and well-known personal growth experts, including:

- Nathaniel Branden—author of over 20 books and considered by many the father of the concept of self-esteem
- Jack Canfield—co-author of *Chicken Soup for the Soul* and many others
- Sonia Choquette—author of *Trust Your Vibes and True Balance*
- Arthur Joseph—vocal coach and author of *Vocal Power*
- Arleah Shechtman—co-author of *Love in the Present Tense*
- Chris Howard—author of *Turning Passion into Profits*
- David Riklan—president and co-founder of SelfGrowth.com
- James Ray—author of *The Science of Success*
- Ava Cadell—relationship expert and author of *Passion Power*
- And many more!

Simply visit our special member's bonus page and listen to Scott Martineau's personal message. He'll guide you on how to receive immediate access to the "behind the scenes" interviews. To get to the bonus page go to www.consciousone.com/bonuspage/bonus.cfm. The bonus content is available only for purchasers of the book and is available only via the Internet.

---

*As an additional bonus we have included video content and interviews from ConsciousOne.com authors and contributors. To access the video content go to www.consciousone.com/bonuspage/bonus.cfm.